The Practice of Waiting on God

THE PRACTICE OF WAITING ON GOD

✠ ✠ ✠

JACK CHOW

Milton Keynes, UK

AuthorHouse™
1663 Liberty Drive, Suite 200
Bloomington, IN 47403
www.authorhouse.com
Phone: 1-800-839-8640

AuthorHouse™ UK Ltd.
500 Avebury Boulevard
Central Milton Keynes, MK9 2BE
www.authorhouse.co.uk
Phone: 08001974150

First published by AuthorHouse 3/7/2006

ISBN: 1-4208-8347-X (e)
ISBN: 1-4208-8346-1 (sc)
ISBN: 1-4208-8345-3 (dj)

Library of Congress Control Number: 2005908051

Printed in the United States of America
Bloomington, Indiana

This book is printed on acid-free paper.

This book is dedicated to

Nancy, my loving wife, best friend and co-laborer,

our adult children and grandchildren,

and

all those who earnestly seek to know God

and desire above all things

to build up their personal and intimate relationship with God.

TABLE OF CONTENTS

✠ ✠ ✠

Chapter One

WHAT THE BIBLE SAYS ABOUT WAITING ON GOD

✠ ✠ ✠

THE BIBLE HAS A LOT TO SAY about waiting on God. It also teaches about silence and stillness before God. We read, first of all, these instructions in the Old Testament: "Be silent before the Sovereign Lord," "Let all the [people on] earth be silent before Him," "Be still and know that I am God," "Be still before the Lord, all mankind, because He has roused Himself from His holy dwelling."[1] These are some of the specific commands of God who would have all humanity turn to Him, learn to be silent and still before Him, and be instructed and blessed by Him. These commands are tantamount to a divine invitation to come to God so He may bestow upon us the blessings He has in store for us. Ours is a God who always desires to bless His people.

We read in Isaiah 30:15-18 (NKJV): "For thus says the Lord God, the Holy One of Israel, 'in returning and rest you shall be saved; in quietness and confidence shall be your strength…The Lord will wait that He may be gracious to you. Blessed are all those who wait for Him.'" In verse 18, the NIV translation has this additional blessed thought: "The Lord *longs* to be gracious to you." The Lord invites and

---

[1] Zephaniah 1:7a, Habakkuk 2:20b, Psalm 46:10, Zechariah 2:13 (All Bible references are taken from the New International Version unless otherwise indicated.)

waits for us to come to Him and even *longs* to show us His love and compassion.

Further on, we read, "He gives power to the weak, and to those who have no might He increases strength...Those who wait on the Lord shall renew their strength; they shall mount up with wings like eagles, they shall run and not be weary, they shall walk and not faint." (Isaiah 40:29, 31NKJV) To those who would wait on God, the promise is certain: They shall not lack power or strength on the journey that leads to eternity.

Listen to this reassuring call from the Savior who understands our weaknesses: "Since we have a great high priest who has gone through the heavens, Jesus the Son of God, let us hold firmly to the faith we profess. For we do not have a high priest who is unable to sympathize with our weaknesses, but we have one who has been tempted in every way just as we are—yet was without sin. Let us then *approach* the throne of grace [for Jesus is full of grace] *with confidence* so that we may receive mercy and find grace to help us in our time of need." (Hebrews 4:15-16)

Going On To Maturity

The writer of Hebrews goes on to urge Christians, who apparently are spiritually immature and seemingly wearied, to "leave the elementary teachings about Christ and go on to maturity"—to know Jesus Christ in all His fullness. At least seven times in this epistle, whose real author is the Holy Spirit, we hear the Lord calling His people in varying ways to "draw near to God." But how do we draw near to God? We all know that God is in heaven, but how many of us know that God also resides, by His Spirit, in the deep recesses of our hearts and souls? God is actually closer to us than we realize. As born-again and Spirit-filled Christians, we know that God dwells in the very depths of our souls. We are God's dwelling place on earth. So to draw close to God is to withdraw from outward things and turn our hearts toward God. Silence coupled with simple faith is the key to entering into the presence of God.

"Be still before the Lord and wait patiently for Him." (Psalm 37:7a) We are called to practice stillness and silence before the Lord. We are to learn to wait on God in patience and restfulness, free from anxiety or uneasiness. The KJV Bible thus renders this verse: "Rest in the Lord [or "Be silent to the Lord" as in the margin] and wait patiently for Him." "For evildoers shall be cut off, but those that wait upon the Lord, they shall inherit the earth [or partake of the riches of God]." (Psalm 37:9NKJV)

Be Still and Know God

"Be still and know that I am God." (Psalm 46:10a) This powerful verse may mean different things to different people, but to me personally, it has meant variously: "relax," "calm down," "be quiet," "quit struggling," "stop trying in your strength," "leave it to the Lord," "trust in God," and "believe that God is still on the throne." This is how the Lord has spoken to me on various occasions through this particular verse.

In the midst of storms, instead of becoming upset or fearful, the Holy Spirit has taught me to just get quiet and still before the Lord and believe that God is in charge. This has pulled me through some of the most difficult and challenging situations I have faced in my life and ministry!

In times of uncertainty and insecurity, we can always draw near to God and put our trust in Him, simply believing that He is in control of every situation!

The Men and Women Who Waited on God

Let us look at some of the outstanding men and women in the Bible to see how they were blessed as they waited on the Lord—spending their time in the presence of God.

King David, whose psalms have blessed many of God's people throughout the generations, knew well the secret of waiting on God in silence and stillness. He knew how to touch the heart of God because he learned the secret of being alone with God. He understood what is and what is not pleasing to God. God Himself testified of him: "I have found David a man after my own heart; he will do everything I want him to do." David indeed "served God's purpose in his own generation." (Acts 13:22,36)

David Always Waited on the Lord

Moreover, David had a singleness of heart and an insatiable desire for God. He writes, "My soul thirsts for God, for the living God. When can I go and meet with God?" "One thing I ask of the Lord," says David, "this is what I seek: that I may dwell in the house of the Lord all the days of my life to gaze upon the beauty of the Lord, and to seek Him in His temple." (Psalms 42:2, 27:4)

Whether he was dwelling in the house of the Lord and gazing upon the Lord's beauty, or attending to his nation's business, King David always waited on the Lord and desired to live daily in His presence. We have every reason to believe that he had spent much of his lifetime lingering in the presence of the Lord—seeking God's face.

David understood the secret of "gazing upon the beauty of the Lord." This is a deep, deep spiritual exercise of the soul in delighting oneself in the goodness and perfections of the Lord. He also understood the intrinsic value of silence and stillness while waiting on the Lord. He writes, "Truly my soul waiteth upon God [or "my heart waits *silently* and *only* upon God" as in the Chinese Union Version]: from Him cometh my salvation. He only is my rock and my salvation; He is my defence; I shall not be greatly moved." (Psalm 62:1-2KJV)

David would remind himself of the need to wait on God by saying, "My soul, wait thou [*silently* and] *only* upon God, for my expectation is from Him." He prays to God, "Yea, let none that wait on Thee be ashamed… Show me Thy ways, O Lord, teach me Thy paths… for Thou art the God of my salvation, on Thee do I wait all day long." Knowing the enormous value of waiting on God, David makes this passionate plea: "Wait on the Lord. Be of good courage, and He shall strengthen thine heart. Wait, I say, on the Lord." (Psalms 62:5, 25:3a, 4-5, 27:14KJV)

Isaiah Waited On God Daily

Besides David, the prophet Isaiah is another outstanding example of a man who daily practiced the ancient art of waiting on God. He found this godly practice to be the source of his strength and wisdom as a servant of God. He says, "The Lord wakens me morning by morning, [He] wakens my ear like one being taught." (Isaiah 50:4b) How Isaiah waited upon the Lord morning by morning and listened as God spoke to him and then through him—even to this day! The apostle John tells us that Isaiah "saw Jesus' glory and spoke about Him." (John 12:41)

Jesus the Son of God apparently revealed His glory to the prophet of old as he waited on the Lord daily. During his quiet times, the prophet also found out that "the Lord *longs* to be gracious" to His people. He himself was much blessed by his waiting on God day in and day out. Thus he declares, "Blessed are all they that wait for Him...they that wait upon the Lord shall renew their strength." (Isaiah 30:18d; 40:31aKJV)

Jeremiah Got Alone with God

Jeremiah is another Old Testament figure who knew the blessedness of solitude—alone with God. He chose fellowship with God over social engagements. He says, "I never sat in the company of revelers, never made merry with them." As he "sat alone" in the presence of God, the word of the Lord came to him profusely, and he enjoyed it so much that he literally "ate" God's words as they came to him. He told the Lord, "When your words came, I ate them; they were my joy and my heart's delight." (Jeremiah 15:16-17)

As we read the books of the prophets in the Old Testament, we find that they all have one thing in common: The word of the Lord came to them as they waited on God. If Christians today would choose to spend time alone with God and learn to wait on God quietly and patiently, as the prophets of old did, they, too, would hear God speak. "For God does not show favoritism." (Romans 12:11) Ever since creation God has desired to communicate His thoughts to His people and to have fellowship with them.

But how can we hear God speak unless we come close to Him—close enough to hear that still small voice of the Spirit of God that dwells within us? How do we know what God has to say to us and to the world unless we take time to wait upon Him and read and meditate over His Word? The practice of waiting on God is one essential way of drawing near to God in order to hear His voice.

All Christians May Hear God Speak

As New Testament believers, we have the privilege of coming to God to hear Him speak firsthand. We don't have to be a prophet in order to hear God. We can hear God speak to us simply by getting quiet and still before Him, giving Him our undivided attention, and reading and meditating over His Word. But many Christians would have only the prophets speak to them primarily because they are unfamiliar with the Scriptures and unlearned in the way of waiting on God. Yet the writer of Hebrews tells us plainly at the outset: "In the past God spoke to our forefathers through the prophets at many times and in various ways, but in these last days He has spoken to us by His Son," i.e. by the living Word and the Spirit of Christ that dwells within us. In other words, in these New Testament times, God speaks to us directly by His Son who is the living Word that once became flesh but now lives in our hearts by His Holy Spirit.

Speaking of the New Testament believers, the Lord says, "I will put my laws in their minds and write them on their hearts. I will be their God and they will be my people. No longer will a man teach his neighbor, or a man his brother, saying, 'know the Lord,' because they will *all* know me, from the least of them to the greatest." (Hebrews 8:10-11) We will *all* know God. This is what God has promised *all* believers in New Testament times. And this is what the practice of waiting on God is all about.

Some New Testament Examples

The first perfect example we see in the New Testament is, of course, our Lord Jesus. The hallmark of Jesus' earthly life and ministry was being with God the Father alone—whenever and wherever possible. We read in the Gospels how Jesus would often withdraw to a quiet solitary place just to pray—to wait on God. He did so even in the midst of a grueling ministry. Once at Capernaum, hometown of Peter, Jesus had already spent a busy day teaching and ministering to the sick and demon-possessed in the synagogue. Later in the evening, after the Lord healed Peter's mother-in-law in his home, "the whole town gathered at the door," and "the people brought to Jesus all the sick and demon-possessed and Jesus healed many who had various diseases. He also drove out many demons." Yet, as Mark notes, "very early in the morning, while it was still dark, Jesus got up, left the house and went off to a solitary place where he prayed." (Mark 1:30-34) Further on, Mark records, "*Every* evening, Jesus went out of the city"—apparently to a solitary place for His regular tryst with the Father (Mark 11:19 Chinese Union Version).

We have reasons to believe that Jesus began His prayer life early in life as a child. At the age of 12, Luke records, Jesus had a burden for His "Father's business." Although Jesus did not begin His public ministry until He was about 30 years of age, the Bible is silent about what He did during those 18 years. Nevertheless, there is every reason to believe that besides working in the carpenter's shop, Jesus studied the Scriptures diligently, prayed much, and undoubtedly spent a considerable amount of time waiting on God.

A Balanced Life and Ministry

We see in Jesus also a perfect example of a busy public ministry balanced with a private prayer life and time for physical rest. Jesus taught His disciples about the need for a proper balance between ministry and relaxation. For instance, when the twelve disciples returned from a missionary trip filled with excitement over the many miracles they had done, they "gathered around Jesus and reported to Him all they had done and taught." "Then," Mark notes pointedly, "because so many people were coming and going that they did not even have a chance to eat, He said to them, 'Come with me by yourselves to a *quiet* place and get some *rest*.' So they went away by themselves in a boat to a *solitary* place"—just to be with Jesus (Mark 6:30-32).

Here is an important lesson for all of us to learn, especially those of us in ministry and leadership positions: We need to maintain a balance between public life/ministry and private prayer life and rest. For married ministers with family obligations, there are three areas of personal life at risk of neglect because of ministry demands. These are our marriage relationship, family life, and personal devotional life. As ministers and church leaders, we must not neglect these three vital areas of our life, or we will fail in both public life and ministry. We must make time for our spouse and family, and for our personal spiritual growth through self-education—digging into God's Word and reading good soul-nourishing books—and a consistent private prayer life.

According to one recent estimate, approximately 15% of clergy suffer from burnout—exhaustion to the point of malfunction—as opposed to 8-12% among the general population. This is a wake-up call for busy clergy and lay people and busy Christians to slow down! As Christians, we are supposed to be the happiest and healthiest people on the face of the earth! And we are to keep it that way.

The Example of Paul

The apostle Paul is another example of maintaining a balance between public ministry and private prayer life. He had gone on three missionary journeys of historic proportions and established numerous churches in Europe and Asia Minor. Despite the vicissitudes of his life and ministry, Paul was a man continually living in Christ and Christ in him. He was one with Christ as Jesus was one with the Father.

Writing to the Christians in Galatia, Paul declares, "I no longer live, but Christ lives in me." To the Philippians, he writes, "For to me, to live is Christ." Addressing the Colossians, Paul instructs, "Just as you received Christ Jesus as Lord, continue to live in Him." Writing to the Thessalonians, he exhorts, "Whether we are awake or asleep, we may live together with Him." He taught them to "pray continually" and the Ephesians to "pray in the Spirit on all occasions with all kinds of prayers...and always keep on praying for all the saints." Paul was truly a man of prayer and in constant fellowship with God.

In his letter to the Galatians, Paul recalls that immediately after his conversion, he had retreated into the Arabian wilderness where he probably spent a better part of three years waiting on the Lord. It was probably during his quiet times there that he had had the experience of being "caught up to the third heaven," hearing what he termed "inexpressible things" and receiving "surpassingly great revelations" concerning the mystery of Christ. (See Galatians 1:15-18, II Corinthians 12:2,4,7.)

THE PROPHETESS ANNA

In the New Testament, we also find an eighty-four-year-old prophetess whose name was Anna. She had been married for seven years and then became a widow (or a widow for eighty-four years). She spent practically all her widowed life living in the presence of God. "She never left the temple but worshiped [God] night and day, fasting and praying," Luke records. When the baby Jesus was brought into the temple, "she gave thanks to God and spoke about the child to all who were looking forward to the redemption of Jerusalem." (Luke 2:36-38) Anna received the Good News apparently through divine revelation while she was praying and waiting on God during those long years.

THE STORY OF MARY AND MARTHA

Last but not least, the story of Mary and Martha (Luke 10:38-42). It is told time and again, but its spiritual significance might still not be fully grasped by many Christians. The picture of Mary sitting at Jesus' feet and listening to His word is a familiar and beautiful one. But we must ask this question: What is the lesson that the Holy Spirit is trying to teach us through this little story that Luke was inspired to record? It is simply this: Spending time on our knees before the Lord and listening to what He has to say to us is far more important than just ministering or serving the Lord and His people. Sitting at Jesus' feet or waiting on the Lord is probably the most essential part of Christian service.

INTIMACY WITH GOD MUST COME FIRST

In the mind of the Lord, it is not service or work for Him that comes first; it is intimacy with Him—spending time in His presence—that comes first. But too often we have this order of priority reversed! We would do well to remember this: Our personal relationship with Christ must come first and before everything and everyone else! God must be first and foremost in our heart, mind and life! The early church at Ephesus made the mistake of forsaking their "first love," i.e. not maintaining a loving relationship with Jesus at all times. She had to be rebuked and told to repent (Revelation 2:2-5). God desires not just *workers,* but more importantly, *lovers.* Martin Luther once said,

"With God, one lover is better and more pleasing to Him than 100,000 hirelings. This also applies to their outward actions."

It is often said that Christianity is not a religion (i.e., not just church attendance, words, rituals and programs). It is instead a relationship—a personal loving relationship with Jesus Christ our Lord. It is a vital relationship. For Christ is literally everything we need in our life—He is indeed our very life! Christ is not only our Lord and Savior but also the coming Bridegroom, therefore, a loving relationship with Him—or a *lovership,* if you will—must be maintained until He comes for His Bride who is the Church.

Things That Really Matter

Another point needs to be made. As far as God is concerned, it is not what we say or do that matters; it is the way we live our Christian life—both in private and in public—that matters. Also, it is not what we say or do that counts; it is what God says and does *in* and *through* us that counts. The Preacher says, "I know that everything God does will endure forever; nothing can be added to it and nothing taken from it." (Ecclesiastes 3:14)

In the sight of God, what we are is by far more important than what we do or say. As Watchman Nee put it: "God attaches greater importance to what we *are* than what we *do*; true ministry is a natural outflow of the life of Christ within; the service that counts in God's sight is living out the life of Jesus. Consecration does not mean necessarily working for God, but rather letting God work freely in us; those who do not let God work in them cannot work for Him."

Knowing What Is Important To God

In our Christian service and ministry, it is absolutely essential that we know what is important *to God*, not just what is important to us. For what is important to us may not be important to God at all. God says, "For my thoughts are not your thoughts, neither are your ways my ways." (Isaiah 55:8) When the prophet Samuel was sent to anoint David as God's chosen king of Israel, he found out this one thing: "The Lord does not look at the things man looks at. Man looks at the outward appearance, but the Lord looks at the heart." (1 Samuel 16:7b)

In God's sight, what is on the inside is more important than what is on the outside.

In the modern technological world, it is the state-of-the-art that counts; in the kingdom of God, it is the state-of-the-heart that matters. If our heart is right and our motive is pure before God, what we do and say will be acceptable in God's sight. That is why the Scripture commands, "Above all else, guard your heart, for it is the wellspring of life." Jesus says, "Blessed are the pure in heart, for they will see God." (Proverbs 4:23, Matthew 5:8)

Knowing Which Is More Important

Let us remember also that with God, loving Him is far more important than loving His service or material blessings. It is more important that we are in love with Jesus Himself than with our ministry, spiritual gifts or emotional feelings. It is more important that we spend time with God than with people or than just doing things for Him. The great desire of God's heart is for us to come near to Him and have fellowship with Him. Hardly do we realize that God desires to have fellowship with us more than we do with Him! It is for this reason that we are created—to have fellowship with the Creator. Therefore, we need to learn how to wait on the Lord and have fellowship with Him.

Finding Peace and Rest In God

Our heart will not have peace and rest until it finds peace and rest in God. Likewise, God, the Creator of heaven and earth and all things therein, will not have rest until He finds rest in our soul. This is what God means when He says, "Heaven is my throne, and the earth is my footstool. Where is the house you will build for me? Where will my resting place be? This is the one I esteem: he who is humble and contrite in spirit and trembles at my word." (Isaiah 66:1,2) God's resting place is found in a humble heart and broken spirit—the man and woman who takes His Word seriously. These are the people who know inner peace, inner rest and inner joy.

Now let us look again at Mary and Martha who represent two different categories of Christians. The difference between the two sisters is not that they did not love the Lord; both of them loved Jesus intensely; both of them served the Lord faithfully and sacrificially. The difference lay in their understanding and choice: Martha chose only public service for the Lord, but Mary chose fellowship with Jesus while serving the Lord sacrificially in public. It goes without saying that Jesus needs our service, but He desires our fellowship and obedience even more.

Loving Jesus Himself More Than His Service

In the case of Martha, her heart was occupied with the service of the King rather than the King Himself. Because she knew not the secret of sitting at the feet of Jesus—drinking spiritually at the fountain of living waters—she had no peace and rest; she was "worried" and "upset" because she was serving the Lord in her own way while Mary would do it only as Jesus desired. Serving the Master only as He desires always brings joy, peace and rest!

When Martha came to Jesus complaining about her sister Mary, the Lord quickly but gently rebuked her, saying, "Martha, Martha, you are worried and upset about many things, but only one thing is needed [or "indispensable" as in the Chinese Union Version]. Mary has chosen what is better and it will not be taken away from her." Mary knew the secret of sitting at Jesus' feet; she heard wonderful words of eternal life direct from the lips of the Son of God. Serving the Lord is good, but sitting at Jesus' feet, or intimacy with the Lord, not only pleases Him but also makes us better servants.

Mrs. Alice Reynolds Flower, a spiritual Christian writer and poet, writes, "There must be that personal, precious, peculiar intimacy with Jesus who is the King of kings and Lord of lords. [However,] there has been such unfortunate substitution here by many dear Christians. Take the matter of our service—our labor for Him. It deters us from those vital audience seasons in His presence. Our activities, while intensely active, can become sadly barren and unfruitful. Abiding in Christ, waiting on the Lord, is the requisite for fruitful living and ministry of every sort; abiding in Him implies a constant looking upon His face."

Are there not many Christians today like Martha? Failing to appreciate the value of waiting on the Lord, they have missed the privilege of hearing wonderful things first hand from the Son of God. As God's children, they have unknowingly denied themselves the blood-bought right of approaching "the throne of grace so that we may receive mercy and find grace to help us in our time of need." (Hebrews 4:16) They have missed the blessed opportunity of being taught by the Spirit of Jesus, who is the greatest Teacher of all time! Oh, what wonderful things Jesus of Nazareth had taught His disciples and those who came to hear Him face-to-face! Jesus would do the same for us today if we would make time for our daily rendezvous with Him and learn to wait on the Lord on a regular basis.

In the choice of things, we know the difference between what is "good" and what is "better," and between "the best" and "the second best." Mary was distinctly different from her sister Martha in that she made what might be described as "the very best" choice—fellowship with Jesus and feeding on His Word—while Martha's choice might be called the "second best"—just doing things busily for Jesus. Moreover, the most striking difference between the two sisters is that Mary's heart was occupied with *Jesus* and *His Word* while Martha's heart was concerned with *many things* that even caused her to be "upset." What Martha chose was obviously the second best and temporary; what Mary chose was absolutely the very best and eternal. What is your choice?

Chapter Two

WHAT IS WAITING ON GOD

✠ ✠ ✠

WAITING ON GOD IS A BIBLICAL CONCEPT; it means approaching the Almighty for help or fellowship. The Biblical phrase "waiting on [or upon] the Lord" is used more frequently by David in many of his psalms than by other writers in the Scriptures. The phrase is also found in the books of Isaiah, Jeremiah and some of the Minor Prophets.

According to *Strong's* Concordance, the Hebrew word root for the phrase "wait on" has these derivative connotations: being still, together with, bind together, focus on, looking to, expect from, appropriate, etc. There is a fundamental difference, however, between the Biblical usage of the phrase "wait upon" and the common usage of the words "wait for" as we understand it. For a better understanding of the difference, a simple illustration is in order. When you wait *for* someone, you wait for a person who is yet to come. But when you wait *on* someone, let's say a customer in a store or a restaurant, it simply means that that person is already present on the scene. *So it is with waiting on God.* Therefore, in the Biblical sense of the word, when you wait on God, it means that God is already there with you and for you.

The practice of waiting on God should be recognized as a privilege as well as a tool available for every child of God to use in approaching our gracious Heavenly Father in time of need. To recognize that we are a needy people before God is a healthy attitude in any growing Christian.

Definitions of Waiting On God

Just what is waiting on God? Simply put, it is drawing near to or coming into contact with God; it is coming to meet God face-to-face, spiritually speaking. For young Christians, however, waiting on God is a spiritual practice that will help them get acquainted with the Savior and with His holy presence. It means being with God alone, learning to get quiet and still not only in our body but in our soul and spirit as well, so that we may be able to hear His voice and recognize the Lord who is the Spirit. The practice of waiting on God is an effective way of cultivating our personal and intimate relationship with the Lord.

For the average Christian, however, it may be hard at first glance to grasp the full import of waiting on the Lord, but the Bible clearly tells us that God desires to have communion with His people and even *longs* for us to come near to Him and have fellowship with Him. "Come near to God and He will come near to you." (James 4:8a) This promise is given to every child of God.

Using the love language that we as humans can understand, the Lord thus calls upon every Christian: "Arise, my darling, my beautiful one, and come with me…Arise, come, my darling, my beautiful one, come with me." (Song of Songs 2:10, 13) To those who love the Lord the way He desires by obeying His commandments, Jesus promises, "I will reveal myself to each one of them." (John 14:21NLT)

As noted at the outset, the Biblical usage of the phrase "wait on" implies that when we wait upon the Lord, we are already together with Him—in His presence—even though we may not feel anything physically or emotionally at the time. So it is very important to keep in mind that whenever we engage in the practice of waiting on God—particularly in silence and stillness—we are already in the presence of God; we must believe that we are there *together with* God; whether we feel it or not, we are spiritually and matter-of-factly *bound together* with God.

Waiting on God is the highest form of service a Christian can render to our Savior and Master. As we wait upon the Lord in silence and stillness, we are actually in God's presence and ready to do His bidding as He commands.

Looking Unto Jesus Alone

As we undertake the practice of waiting on God, we are to be focused on the Lord Jesus Himself, "looking unto Jesus [i.e. looking away from everything else, including even our own needs and problems, and focus on Jesus alone], the author and finisher of our faith" (Hebrews 12:2aNKJV), anticipating good things from Him, and appropriating, by faith, all that we are in need of from the One who created all things. If you need peace, for instance, expect the God of peace to give it to you; if you need patience, just ask and receive it from Him by faith; if you need more of God's love, just ask Him to pour it into your heart. Jesus has promised, "Ask and it will be given to you; seek and you will find; knock and the door will be opened to you. For everyone who asks receives, he who seeks finds; and to him who knocks, the door will be opened." (Matthew 7:7,8) This should be our mental attitude and expectation whenever we come to seek the face of God.

It Is Coming to the Fountain of Living Waters

Waiting on God means coming to the One who calls Himself "the fountain of living waters"—signifying that God is the Source of infinite and endless supply, whatever the need, be it wisdom, strength, love, peace, joy, patience, forgiveness, healing, or divine health. Waiting on the Lord means to be connected with the One from whom all blessings flow—the One who has conquered sin, the flesh, the world and the devil so that we as Christians may share the secret of His power and victories.

Waiting on God is basically an internal spiritual practice as well as an exercise of faith. It is a practice that will make us increasingly aware of the presence of God and bring us eventually into a life of living daily and happily in His presence. In the beginning, it may or may not involve emotional feelings, but there is always a sense of peace and tranquility as we get quiet and still *before the Lord.* Such a peaceful atmosphere may be described as a sacred peace and quietness; it means that the God of peace has come near to you and that you are experiencing His holy presence. Such sacred peace and silence usually signify the intangible *manifestation* of the presence of God. When the invisible God comes to us, wonderful things will happen in our soul and life even without our immediate recognition.

Wonderful Things Happen As We Wait On God

When we wait on the Lord in silence and stillness, at least two things will happen to us: 1. We grow—consciously or unconsciously—closer to God, 2. We are transformed from the inside out. Although other wonderful things can also happen as we wait on God, these two things are certain to take place even without our realizing it. But sooner or later we will discover the changes wrought by the indwelling Holy Spirit. This is one of those mysterious ways in which the Spirit of God works in our lives.

God always does something wonderful in our hearts and souls as we spend time in His presence, whether waiting on Him in silence or reading and meditating on His Word. Another thing that God will do for us when we wait upon Him and read and meditate on His Word is that He will cause His words to come alive to us as if God Himself were speaking to us! For God does speak to us through His inspired Word the Bible. But we need to be alert and spiritually sensitive as we wait on God and read His Word.

It Is An Exercise of Faith

Waiting on God is essentially an exercise of faith, believing that we have come into His presence and that He is able to meet our needs as we look up to Him with hope and expectation. For God knows our needs and weaknesses and, as we come to Him, He is always ready to meet our respective need oftentimes in ways that surprise us. But we must have faith in God because "without faith it is impossible to please God." Therefore, as the Bible says, "Anyone who comes to Him must believe that He exists and that He rewards those who earnestly seek Him." (Hebrews 11:6)

As I mentioned before, waiting on God means coming to meet God face-to-face but, as we have just noted, "anyone who comes to Him *must believe*" that He is there for him or her and that "He rewards those who earnestly seek Him." Jesus says, "The man [or woman] who comes to me I will never turn away." (John 6:37bNEB) The Lord *longs* to receive and reward those of us who earnestly seek Him, but again we *must believe* that He is there for us when we draw near to Him.

The psalmist writes, "Better is one day in your courts [or presence] than a thousand elsewhere." This speaks of the immeasurable value and blessedness of spending time in the presence of God—waiting on the Lord. "Blessed is the man [or woman] You choose and cause to approach You, that he [or she] may dwell in Your courts. We shall be satisfied with the goodness of Your house." (Psalm 84:10a, 65:4NKJV)

THE SECRET OF BATHING OUR SOULS

A. W. Tozer, author of numerous books on inner life, described waiting on God in silence and stillness as "bathing our souls in silence." But he said, "Very few of us know the secret of bathing our souls in silence. It was a secret our Lord Jesus knew very well." What is the secret of "bathing our souls in silence?" It is that mysterious yet powerful operation of the Spirit of God upon our souls as we get quiet and still before our Lord—that silent cleansing, purifying and sanctifying of our hearts and souls so that God can fill us more and more with His own holiness and fullness. It is a process of transformation wrought by the Holy Spirit in our lives as we persist in the practice of waiting on God.

LIVING IN THE PRESENCE OF GOD

Waiting on God is a practical way of coming into God's presence; its practice can gradually become a habitual lifestyle for Christian living—living constantly in the presence of God. But we must cultivate such a lifestyle on a continuing basis until we become accustomed to walking and talking with God as an integral part of our daily life. Every born-again and Spirit-filled Christian is entitled to live a life of abiding in the Lord.

Jesus says to all of us, "Remain in me and I will remain in you." This kind of lifestyle has been made possible by God the Spirit who has come to dwell within us. When Jesus spoke of the coming of the Holy Spirit, He made two things perfectly clear: 1. He (the Spirit of truth) will be with us forever, 2. He *lives* with us and is *in* us (see John 14:16-17). In the next verse, Jesus underscores, "I will not leave you as orphans [or alone, uncared for]; I will *come to* you." All these things speak of the abiding presence of God with us in this dispensation of the Holy Spirit. If that's not enough, Jesus' other name Immanuel which means "God with us" should suffice.

When we have Jesus as our personal Savior, we have "God with us"—we have the presence of God with us. This should be a common Christian experience, but this does not seem to be the case in reality with most Christians. And the reason for that is that they have apparently missed the central point of the coming of the Holy Spirit: to make Jesus or the presence of God real and personal in our Christian life. Another reason may be that the importance and value of waiting on God has not been adequately taught.

Every child of God has the privilege of experiencing and living in the presence of God. We do not have to wait until we go to heaven in order to enjoy the presence of God; the presence of the Lord is something that can be obtained here on earth and *now.* For those of us who might still be unfamiliar with the presence of God, we need to practice and cultivate it diligently and regularly. The Holy Spirit who has come to dwell within us will help us to attain it. The Holy Spirit is, in fact, the empowering presence of God in our heart and life! "You will receive power when the Holy Spirit comes on [or dwells in] you." (Acts 1:8)

It Is the Development of Inner Life

Waiting on God in silence and stillness is an internal spiritual exercise; it requires turning our heart, mind, thoughts and feelings toward God Himself. It is an exercise where we turn our attention away from things external and focus internally and solely on the Lord Jesus who dwells within us.

Waiting on God is actually the development of our inner life. It is allowing God to build up our inner being so that we may be strong in our outer life. We cannot live an effective and fruitful outer life unless our inner life—our personal relationship with God—is strong. Therefore, we need to develop a strong inner life—an abiding life in Christ and Christ living in us—through the continuing practice of waiting on God. "I pray that out of His glorious riches He may strengthen you with power through His Spirit in your inner being, so that Christ may dwell in your hearts through faith." (Ephesians 3:16,17a)

Let us remember this powerful call of God: "Be still and know that I am God." (Psalm 46:10a) Being quiet and still before God and *knowing* that He is the Almighty God can be powerful stuff in a Christian's life! Paul reminds the Christians at Corinth: "Christ is not weak toward you, but *mighty in* you." He declares to the Philippians, "I can do all things through Christ who strengthens me." Waiting on God in silence and stillness is an effective way of knowing God better and growing deeper in Him.

It Is Another Form of Deeper Prayer Life

Waiting on God is another form of a deeper prayer life; it is communion or fellowship with God, or developing a personal dialogue with God through the medium of His written Word. It is a two-way communication between God and man. However, when the word "prayer" is mentioned, it is generally understood to be asking God for this or that. But when you practice waiting on God, you develop a kind of prayer where you allow God to talk to you and you learn to just listen. God talks to us only when we hold our peace and listen. There are certain exceptions, of course, but it is usually in quietness and silence that we hear God speak. Waiting on God in silence and stillness may be the best way to develop our ability to hear that "still small voice" of God.

It Is Developing Intimacy With God

Waiting on God is also a way of seeking God's face—to cultivate intimacy with God. As we practice it continuously, it will help us naturally to develop a closer personal relationship with Jesus. We all desire to have intimacy with God, but without the practice of waiting on God, we are not going to get much closer to God or grow deeper in Him. Our desire for God must be intense and pure; we must be single-minded and focused on Jesus as we wait on the Lord. Jesus—Jesus alone—must be first and foremost on our minds and in our hearts at all times. Thus, the practice of waiting on God will certainly help strengthen and deepen our relationship with the Lord and increase our empirical knowledge of Him.

It Is Allowing God To Do Deeper Work

While we have much to gain by practicing the art of waiting on God, when we do so, we also give God an opportunity to do a deeper and lasting works in our hearts and souls that will be reflected in our Christian walk. It is vitally important that we allow God sufficient time to finish the good work He has begun in our respective lives. In order that God may accomplish His plans for our lives, we need to spend more time with Him so that He may work out His eternal purposes in our lives.

In the modern business world, time equals money; but in the kingdom of God, time is even more precious than money, because money lost can be regained but time lost can mean the loss of life eternal! God needs our time more than our money or manual labor.

In our busy world, it seems that most of us have time for so many things—secular as well as non-secular—but so few of us have time for God, supposedly the most important person in our life. Very few of us spend time with our loving Father alone. If you love someone, you like to spend time with that person; you want to be alone with him/her if you are in love. God needs our time, the more the better, so He can show us how much He loves us and fulfill His eternal purposes in our lives.

God desires to have fellowship with us, and more significantly, God delights to reveal Himself to us, but we need to give Him our precious time—time to be alone with Him, time to wait upon Him, time to seek His face, and time to delve into His Word. We also need to spend quality time with our loved ones and with those Christians who earnestly seek the Lord. Without making time for waiting on God and studying His Word, it is impossible to know God and have a deep meaningful relationship with Him.

Chapter Three

WHY WE SHOULD WAIT ON GOD

✠ ✠ ✠

THERE ARE MANY REASONS WHY WE SHOULD wait on God. Among them are these: we *need* God, especially in these troubled times; we also need to grow spiritually and be made strong in the Lord. Growing spiritually means knowing God better and having a deepening personal relationship with Him. God commands that we draw near to Him. God desires that we as His children should come to Him, and have fellowship with Him, just as little children come to their father. God delights to be with His people and longs to reveal Himself to them. When we take time to wait on the Lord, we have everything to gain and nothing to lose.

We Need God At All Times

Seldom, if ever, do we realize our need for God when things are going well in our life. But when we find ourselves in tight places or trials in life, we realize how much we need Him and how weak and powerless we are! We do not realize how vulnerable and fragile we are as humans until a tragedy or a serious illness strikes. The terrorist attacks of September 11, 2001 brought home this poignant point in the most painful way.

As the twin towers of the World Trade Center in New York went down and the Pentagon was attacked, thousands of lives were lost and the nation was in shock. Almost instantaneously, our entire nation turned to God for comfort and strength. Signs of "God Bless America" suddenly appeared everywhere, implicitly yet publicly acknowledging our need for God's protection.

As we embark on the journey of waiting upon the Lord, we will soon discover that God indeed is the Source of our strength and courage and all we ever need in our lives.

God, who has loved us with an everlasting love, always desires to bless us—not to harm us. *"For I know the plans I have for you," declares the Lord, "plans to prosper you and not to harm you, plans to give you hope and a future. Then you will call upon me and come and pray to me, and I will listen to you. You will seek me and find me when you seek me with all your heart."* (Jeremiah 29:11-13)

We should wait on the Lord because He has plans to prosper us, both spiritually and materially, and to give us hope for the future. God alone holds and dictates our future. God also promises that when we seek Him with all our heart, we will find Him. A godly woman has defined seeking God this way: "To desire Him is to seek Him, to seek Him is to find Him, to find Him is [or means] everything." As we take time to wait on God, He will give us a greater desire and hunger for Him.

We should wait on the Lord because we love Him as He has loved us with an unconditional and unchanging love. If you truly love someone, you want to spend time with that person, however busy you might be.

To Know the Unsearchable Riches of Christ

Another reason we should wait on God is that our spiritual life is enhanced and enriched as we spend time with God and in His Word. God will unveil His hidden riches and resources for us as He did for the apostle Paul and those who waited on the Lord in times past. Paul, who knew "the unsearchable riches of Christ," testifies: "[God] was pleased to reveal His Son in me so that I might preach Him among the Gentiles." He says, "Although I am less than the least of all God's people, this grace was given me: to preach the unsearchable riches of Christ." (Galatians 1:16, Ephesians 3:8)

If you think you are less than the least of all God's people, you, too, can and will know something about "the unsearchable riches of Christ" as you pursue the practice of waiting on God diligently and faithfully.

Perhaps the most cogent—and glorious—reason we should wait on God is that He desires to change us and make us more like His Son Jesus Christ. "For those God foreknew He also predestined to be conformed to the likeness of His Son, that He might be the firstborn among many brothers." (Romans 8:29) To become like Jesus is the highest point in our salvation and the greatest of all blessings God can bestow upon any man or woman.

Since God has much more in store for us, we should never be satisfied with merely being saved—knowing only that we are going to be in heaven someday. It is good to know where we came from and where we are going, but there is so much more in Christianity. Praying, reading the Bible and going to church are all important and necessary, but there is more. What is more is that we can know Christ better and possess Him in a personal and empirical way.

Jesus says, "I have come that they [meaning those who believe] may have life, and that they may have it more abundantly." (John 10:10bNKJV) In order for us to know Jesus better and possess Him more, we need to seek and pursue after God—i.e. to spend time in His presence and wait upon Him.

We need to learn to wait on the Lord, particularly in silence and solitude, so that we may have Jesus Christ revealed in us by the Spirit of God, and that we may be changed inwardly "from glory to glory"—i.e. to be increasingly transformed into the likeness of the Son of God! God Himself *will* do this for us as we keep up the practice of waiting upon Him.

We Need to Grow Deeper In God

As Christians, we need to grow deeper and be firmly established in the Lord, like a house built on the rock. The way to achieve this is by waiting on the Lord and being fed on His Word on a regular basis. Then, when testing times and trials come upon us, we can stand—and stand firmly.

Many Christians claim to have been born again and filled with the Holy Spirit, but they do not seem to know much about the mighty power of the risen Savior living in them. They readily acknowledge that Jesus died for them on the cross and rose from the dead on the third day; they think that as long as they just "believe" in Jesus that way, they are on their way to heaven, regardless of how they live their lives here on earth. But that is not what the Bible says.

According to the Bible, the Gospel of Jesus Christ not only offers a safe passage to heaven but, more significantly, it brings about a revolutionary change in the life of a born-again believer. The Bible speaks of "putting off the old self" and "putting on the new self"—replacing the old man with the new man like the Son of God. (Ephesians 4:22-24) For this reason, the Apostle Paul says, "I am not ashamed of the Gospel, because it is the power of God for the salvation [and transformation] of everyone who believes." (Romans 1:16)

Is Christ Living In Your Heart?

Is Jesus Christ living in your heart? Have you changed since Jesus came into your heart? If you are a genuinely born-again Christian, your answer to these crucial questions will unequivocally be "yes." With the practice of waiting on God, the reality of Christ living in your heart will only increase as time goes on. As you get quiet and still in the presence of God, the Holy Spirit will work so that the life of Christ that is in you will grow in measure—Christ will become increasingly real and precious to your heart and soul. This being the case, you will have no doubt that Christ is living in your heart!

Another compelling reason why we should wait on God is this: We will be automatically empowered by the Spirit of God as we are connected to the One who is the Source of all power, for it is in Him only that we are strengthened and renewed day by day, thus being able to live a powerful and victorious Christian life in this dark world—free from sin. John the Apostle states emphatically: "Whoever abides in Him does not sin." (1 John 3:6aNKJV)

Jesus Christ is still alive today. The Bible clearly tells us that Jesus rose from the dead and appeared to His disciples in various ways for forty days before He ascended to heaven, giving "many convincing proofs that He was alive." Ten days later, on the day of Pentecost, Jesus poured out the promised Holy Spirit upon all His disciples, filling them and empowering them as well as dwelling in their hearts! The Jesus of Nazareth who had been with them physically for three and half years was now living in them by His Holy Spirit! What mighty changes came to these disciples! These men and women, about 120 of them, had waited on the Lord before they were so filled and indwelled by the Spirit of Christ.

Today this same Jesus who sits on the most honored throne in heaven also lives in our hearts! This should be the experience of every Christian who claims to have been born again and filled with the Holy Spirit. Yet many of us do not seem to live in the power and victory of Christ as we should. By waiting on God, however, the reality of Christ living in our hearts will be realized and increased, and we will be awakened to the fact that the indwelling Christ "is not weak, but *mighty in you*," as Paul reminds the Christians at Corinth. John also tells us: "He [Christ] who is *in you is greater* than he who is in the world." (2 Corinthians 13:3, 1 John 4:4NKJV)

We should take time to wait on the Lord so that we may know Christ and the power of His resurrection as He is revealed in us by the Spirit of God, thereby enabling us to live a happy and overcoming Christian life and, at the same time, to be effective Christian witnesses in the world.

Nonetheless, many Christians who claim to have been saved do not seem to have grown much spiritually, even though they go to church, pray, and read the Bible regularly. They have hardly shown any signs of real change in their behavior or lifestyle. Something seems to be missing in their Christian life.

The fact that these Christians have not grown deeper is probably due to lack of Biblical teaching about waiting on God—something that is so vitally crucial to their spiritual growth and depth. This is perhaps why we do not find much spiritual depth in Christianity today.

Needless to say, it is important that we attend a strong Bible-believing church, pray, and read our Bible daily. But more importantly, we need to set aside time for the specific purpose of waiting on God—reading and meditating on His Word as well as learning to hear and obey God's voice. As we continue to do so daily, we are bound to grow stronger and deeper in the knowledge and the grace of our Lord Jesus.

TO FIND PEACE AND REST IN GOD

Still another reason for us to wait on the Lord is that we may find true peace and rest in Him. "You will keep him in perfect peace whose mind is stayed on You." (Isaiah 26:3NKJV) Isaiah found this "perfect peace" as he waited on the Lord and had his mind fixed on Him morning by morning. He discovered by experience that waiting on God was a sure way of calming his spirit and renewing his strength.

It is during our quiet and peaceful waiting on the Lord that our strength—both spiritual and physical—is renewed and our lives marvelously transformed. This is one of those mysterious ways of the Holy Spirit working in the hearts of those who believe in the truth of waiting on God and practice it faithfully.

As we focus on the Lord Jesus and have our mind and thoughts fixed on Him while waiting on God, we will eventually enter that divine peace and rest which the Lord has promised. Hebrews 4:9-10 says, "There remains a Sabbath-rest for the people of God; for anyone who enters God's rest also rests from his own work." In other words, those who will trust the Lord wholeheartedly as they wait on Him will be ushered into God's rest. The writer of Hebrews thus encourages us: "Let us, therefore, make every effort to enter that rest." (Hebrews 4:11a) As we make every effort to spend time waiting on the Lord, God Himself will in His own way bring us into that divine rest.

God Alone Is Our Resting Place

Moses, the man who knew God face-to-face, tells us that God has been "our dwelling [or resting] place throughout all generations." (Psalm 90:1) It is in God that we find our lasting peace and rest. God alone is the resting place for the human heart and soul. This has been the case "throughout all generations!"

St. Augustine said, "man was made to find his home in God, and he cannot rest until he finds his home in God." We will find our inner peace and rest as we take time to wait on God. David sought the Lord and waited on Him "all the days of (his) life" because, as he said, "My soul finds rest in God alone; my salvation comes from Him." (Psalm 27:4; 62:1)

Yes, God alone is the resting place for our heart and soul! We cannot find true peace and rest until we find them in God. On the other hand, man is a resting place for God as much as God is a resting place for man. But God cannot dwell and rest in our soul until we turn to Him, seek His face, and love Him with all our heart, with all our soul, and with all our mind as the Lord commands.

God says, "Heaven is my throne, and the earth is my footstool. Where will my resting place be? This is the one I esteem: he [or she] who is humble and contrite in spirit, and trembles at my word.'" (Isaiah 66:1-2) It is in men and women who are humble and contrite in spirit and who take God's Word seriously and fearfully that God finds His rest and satisfaction. God will instill in us His divine humility and a godly fear for Him and His Word only as we take time to wait on the Lord faithfully.

WE ARE LIVING IN "TERRIBLE TIMES"

We are living in what the Bible calls "terrible times in the last days." The signs of Christ's second coming foretold in the Scriptures are increasing left and right. Violence is on the rise at home and abroad. Terrorism has become a new form of international threat. Truck bombs and suicide bombers (explosives strapped around human bodies), unheard of before, are a new phenomenon in armed conflicts in various parts of the world. Shootings in public places and homes have become almost a familiar scene. Random killings have occurred even in places of worship in Christian America as well as in Muslim countries. Ironically, lawlessness is rampant as more and more new laws are enacted.

Meanwhile, as far as I (at age 74) can remember, I have never seen so many natural disasters and accidents in the world where people have died not by the hundreds, but by the thousands or tens of thousands. People do not seem to have a sense of security or certainty. Nobody knows what will happen next. Security seems to be a rare commodity these days. If ever we needed God, it is NOW! Where can we flee but to God for security and protection in these uncertain times? If there was ever a time we needed to come closer to God, it is NOW!

GOD ALONE IS OUR REFUGE

It behooves us to draw near to God and learn to wait upon and abide in the Lord, because "God is our refuge and strength, an ever-present help in trouble." David, who probably faced more dangers in his life than any other character in the Bible, said, "He alone is my rock and my salvation; He is my fortress, I will never be shaken. He is my mighty rock, my refuge...Trust *in Him at all times,* O people; pour out your hearts to Him, for God is our refuge." (Psalms 46:1, 62:2,7-8)

In perilous times like these, there is no better place to find peace and security than in the Almighty God who alone holds our future. God alone is able to protect and deliver us from evil. Who knows what the future holds but our Mighty God and Everlasting Father? For God "rules forever by His power, His eyes watch the nations" and "the government will be on His shoulders." (Psalm 66:7, Isaiah 9:6) Should Jesus tarry, we know we can go on singing:

Because He lives, I can face tomorrow,
Because He lives, all fear is gone;
Because I know He holds the future;
And life is worth the living,
Just because He lives.

✠ ✠ ✠

Man Is But Dust and Ashes

Abraham was a man who had a close personal relationship with God. He became known as "God's friend." Abraham knew God and also knew himself, recognizing that he was nothing but dust and ashes. Knowing God and oneself is probably the highest form of science in the universe. General Douglas A. MacArthur of World War II fame prayed this prayer for his son: "Build me a son, O Lord, who will... know Thee—and that to know himself is the foundation stone of knowledge." The true knowledge of God and oneself comes only from the enlightenment of the Spirit of Christ "in whom are hidden all the treasures of wisdom and knowledge." (Colossians 2:3)

Pondering over the greatness and goodness of God, David exclaimed in amazement: "What is man that you are mindful of him, the son of man that you care for him?" (Psalm 8:4) What is man? Man is but dust and ashes, as Abraham said of himself. Man's life is but a breath. A man's life ends with the breathing of his last breath.

"Now listen," says James, the Lord's brother, "you who say, 'Today or tomorrow we will go to this or that city, spend a year there, carry on business and make money.' Why, you do not even know what will happen tomorrow. What is your life? You are a mist that appears for a little while and then vanishes." (James 4:13-14)

While extolling the goodness and mercy of the Lord, David remembered how God "has compassion on those who fear Him," just like a father having compassion on his children, "for He knows how we are formed, He remembers that we are dust." (Psalm 103:13-14)

Coming to God's Throne Is A Privilege

As the redeemed people of God, we are given free access to the throne of God, not because of our own merits but because of the precious blood of Jesus; we in ourselves are unworthy of anything from God. So it is a great privilege to come into the presence of God to wait upon Him, a privilege for which our Lord Jesus paid a high price of His own blood. We must not take this for granted, but avail ourselves of every opportunity to come to God's throne "with confidence so that we may receive mercy and find grace to help us in our time of need."

The writer of Hebrews goes on to encourage us with these words: "Brothers [and sisters], since we have confidence to enter the Most Holy Place [i.e. the presence of God] by the blood of Jesus, by the new and living way opened for us through the curtain, that is, His body, and since we have a great priest over the house of God, *let us draw near to God* with a sincere heart in full assurance of faith." (Hebrews 4:16,10:19-22)

In spite of our human frailties and failures, God still desires for us to come near to Him and learn to wait on Him so that we may know Him and be transformed into the likeness of His Son Jesus Christ. God delights in our knowledge of Him more than the offerings and sacrifices we bring to Him. God *longs* for intimacy with us. God offers us an open door to His throne room. We have God's standing invitation to walk in to have fellowship with Him or receive help in our time of need.

"As God's fellow workers," Paul says, "we urge you not to receive God's grace in vain. For He says, 'In the time of my favor I heard you, and in the day of salvation I helped you.' I tell you, now is the time of God's favor, now is the day of salvation." (2 Corinthians 6:1-2)

Chapter Four

HOW DO WE WAIT ON GOD

✠ ✠ ✠

THIS CHAPTER ON HOW TO WAIT ON God is not intended to be a manual like the one for physical exercise that tells you how to take steps one, two, three in terms of gestures and movements. It is merely an attempt, following Biblical teachings as well as offering some practical suggestions, to help guide you into a deeper and richer relationship with God through the practice of waiting on Him.

As I mentioned before, the practice of waiting on God is basically a spiritual and mental exercise; it would be meaningless if it were treated as a physical or superficial religious exercise. Waiting upon the Lord is truly a faith-based godly exercise. If carried out faithfully and persistently, the exercise will assuredly strengthen and enrich your spiritual life. But it requires absolute faith and the devotion of the heart and soul more than the intellect.

In order for this practice to be successful, one has to have an intense passion for the Lord, a genuine desire to know Him better, and a strong will to develop a personal and intimate relationship with Him. One must also be willing to invest the necessary time that is crucial to the success of the practice. If you wish to profit from the practice of waiting on God, you must allocate time—the more the better. Also, one should not expect quick results, because there is no such thing as "instant success" in the pursuit of godliness and spiritual depth. But patience and perseverance coupled with an unfailing faith will ensure success, since no time will be misspent in waiting on the Lord.

Let me also emphasize that since the success of waiting on God depends primarily on the inner workings of His Holy Spirit, it is important to keep in mind that what God will do for you in this practice is far more important than what you will do for yourself. Faith in God is absolutely necessary in this exercise.

As far as God is concerned, the practice of waiting upon Him will provide an open door for Him to come into your inner being—soul and spirit—to do whatever He deems necessary. God being the all-wise Creator of all things always knows what to do and how to do it. You need only to trust God wholeheartedly and allow Him to do freely what is necessary for you in His own ways. Given time and endurance, you will see the desired results.

> As the Preacher says: *"He has made everything beautiful in its time. He has also set eternity in the hearts of men; yet they cannot fathom what God has done from beginning to end. I know that everything God does will endure forever; nothing can be added to it and nothing taken from it."* (Ecclesiastes 3:11,14)

Putting Your Faith To Work

In talking about waiting on God, the first question usually raised by those interested in the subject is, "What should I do when I wait on the Lord?" My standard answer is this: "Nothing. You do not have to *do* anything. Just come to God with a simple faith and get down before Him. Be quiet and still, believing that you are in His presence and that He is there for you."

God says, "Be still and know that I am God." (Psalm 46:10a) In waiting on the Lord, the first thing you need to know is that you have now come into the presence of the Almighty God, the One who created heaven and earth and all things thereof. We also need to recognize that we are but needy and powerless people who can do nothing without Him.

This correct and acceptable attitude will quickly gain entrance into the Most Holy Place—the deep recesses of our souls and spirits—where God resides. Turn your heart inwardly to God. It is true that God is in heaven. It is equally true that God also dwells by His Spirit in the depths of our hearts and souls. God is actually closer to us than we realize. "Do you not know that your body is a temple of the Holy Spirit who is in you?" (1 Corinthians 6:19a)

St. Augustine once said, "For years and years, I looked for God to come to me from heaven, and then I realized that He is already in me." Every time you come to wait on the Lord, you need to remind yourself that God is already in you—He is already there, desiring to have that personal and sweet fellowship with you. It would be so pleasing to God if you would draw near to Him with such a simple, childlike faith.

DRAWING NEAR TO GOD

You might ask, "What do you mean by drawing near to God? How do I draw near to Him?" You draw near to God *inwardly,* first of all, by turning your heart and mind toward God. You come to God not just with your body but, more importantly, with your heart and soul. If you approach God—who is already in you—with your heart and soul, and with a deep sense of longing and expectation, you will find Him sooner or later.

To wait on the Lord, you need to withdraw to a quiet place, calm down and close your eyes, believing that you have come into the presence of God. If you are a busy person, as most of us are, it may take a little while to get quiet in your soul and spirit as you turn your heart to God who is already in you. If you keep up the practice, you will succeed. Always remember, never look for God *without*; always look for God *within.*

We often sing in church: "Turn your eyes upon Jesus; look full in His wonderful face…" This is just a reminder to look away from outward things and from people around you, and to give your full undivided attention to the One who is within you. Basically, this is how we draw near to God. But it requires a lot of practice—the practice of faith and the exercise of heart.

We draw near to God also by reading and meditating on His Word or simply by being contemplative with our eyes closed. Meditating on the Word of God allows the Spirit of God to impress or "write" His words upon our hearts so that we may live by them. Closing our eyes makes it easier to focus on the Lord. Remember, God is not far from us; He is already in us. Closing our eyes helps bring us closer to God as we turn our hearts to Him. Sometimes, as soon as we close our eyes, we can instantly sense God's nearness; we will find God so close to us—as if we were face-to-face with God.

Learn to talk to God in silence—with your heart. Once you become used to talking to God with your heart, you will feel the touch of God easily. You may also use some good inspirational Christian music and devotional readings to help you focus on God.

The Bible says, "Come near to God and He will come near to you." (James 4:8a) God always means what He says in His Word. So always remember and believe this: Whenever and wherever you draw near to God, He will draw near to you. God who is omnipresent is also in you. So just get alone with God. Get quiet and still before Him. Wait on the Lord patiently. Give Him your loving attention. Tell Him again and again that you love Him. As you do these things, God will presently come near to you.

As you come to wait on God, do not look for feelings or outward manifestations, *but look to Jesus within.* Remind yourself every now and then that Christ is in you. Turn your heart and mind upon Jesus. Keep your internal eyes fixed on Jesus. Think of Jesus more than anything, even the practice itself. Give Him your undivided attention. If you are a busy person, it may take a while for you to calm down and focus on Jesus, but if you keep practicing it, you will feel close to God. This is probably the most effective way of drawing near to God. This is also how we learn to abide in the Lord—to stay attached to Jesus, like the branches attached to a vine.

> Jesus says, *"I am the vine; you are the branches. If a man remains in me and I in him, he will bear much fruit; apart from me you can do nothing."* (John 15:5)

So whenever you come to wait on God, you are spiritually in touch with Him; *you are already in the presence of God.* Waiting on God means actually being in the presence of God and being connected to God who is the Spirit. Since God is the Spirit, He is invisible and untouchable in the physical realm. Spiritually speaking, however, you can *"touch"* God with your heart and *"see"* God with the eyes of your faith. Faith is the only requirement to *"see"* and *"touch"* God. Ask God repeatedly to increase our faith as the apostles did. (Luke 17:5)

Brother Lawrence, whose booklet The Practice of the Presence of God has been a blessing to many Christians, wrote these words toward the end of his life: "I must, in a little time, go to God. What comforts me in this life is that I now *see* Him by faith; and I *see* Him in such a manner as might make me say sometimes, *I believe no more, but I see.*"

As you continue to practice waiting on the Lord, doing your part earnestly and faithfully, God will honor your faith and do His part by coming to you in a way you have never known before. You will eventually become so conscious of the presence of God that wherever you go, you know that God is with you, and ultimately you will find yourself living in the glory of His presence!

Without Faith It Is Impossible to Please God

As I have stated, the practice of waiting on God is basically an exercise of faith—faith based upon Biblical truths. Remember, faith is not feelings or emotion; it is simply believing what God says in His Word the Bible.

For instance, the Bible says, "Come near to God and He will come near to you." If you will just believe and apply it to your heart as you come to wait on the Lord, you will soon develop a sense of God's nearness to you, and you will eventually become increasingly aware of His presence in your heart and life.

Faith is simply to believe what God says in His Word. Faith is powerful stuff, yet it requires no effort on our part—only belief. Read Hebrews 11, the greatest faith chapter in the Bible. The word "faith" is mentioned twenty-five times. All those great men and women of faith, including Enoch and Noah who "walked" with God, were related to God "by faith," and they all lived their lives on earth "by faith."

The Scripture says, "All these people were still living *by faith* when they died. They did not receive the things promised; they only saw them [with the eyes of faith] and welcomed them from a distance." Paul prayed for Christians everywhere "that Christ may dwell in your hearts through faith." (Hebrews 11:13; Ephesians 3:17a)

> *"And without faith, it is impossible to please God, because anyone who comes to Him must believe that He exists and that He rewards those who earnestly seek Him."* (Hebrews 11:6)

Simple faith in the Word of God is the prerequisite of receiving any and every blessing from God. It is the key to enter into the kingdom of God—into the fullness of the blessing of the Gospel. It is faith, instead of feelings or emotion, that thrusts us into the wonderful presence of God. Faith is the shortest way to get into the presence of God and to meet Him face-to-face.

Feelings Versus God Himself

The practice of waiting on God is neither a physical nor an emotional exercise. It is basically an exercise of faith. Therefore, as you begin the practice of waiting on the Lord, you need to be mindful that you are not there to wait for *feelings* but to wait on *God who is already in you.* God must come first. Good feelings will follow at some point, but do not allow your feelings or emotions to take the place of Christ within. *Always look to Jesus within and be focused on Him—Him alone*—as you wait on the Lord.

Do not let your own feelings tell you whether or not God is with you. Feelings are erratic; they come and go. They can be misleading or even deceptive sometimes, but the Word of God is the eternal truth; it never changes. So never allow your own physical or emotional feelings to take the place of the inerrant Word of God. Let the Word of God take precedence over your imagination, opinions and ideas. If the Bible says that God will never leave you nor forsake you, just accept and believe it, whether or not you feel it. "*We live by faith, not by sight* [nor by feelings]." (2 Corinthians 5:7)

The Word of God says, "Those who wait on the Lord shall renew their strength." (Isaiah 40:31aNKJV) That is truth. Stand on it. Whenever you come to wait on the Lord, remind yourself of this promise of God, take it by faith, and expect to be renewed in your strength, or "find new strength," as another translation says.

Let me give you a simple illustration: When you wait on the Lord, you are like a weak or worn-out battery being plugged into a powerful charger; you are being charged up, you are gaining new power! If you wait on God—the Source of power—long enough, you will be filled with power within! If you wait on the Lord every day with such simple faith, you will gain new strength every day! Take God's promise at face value.

Someone asked, "How do you distinguish between your own feelings and the presence of God when you wait on the Lord?" Feelings are human emotional reactions to the presence of God; they are not the presence of God per se, much less God Himself. The presence of God is divine and holy in nature, while our physical and emotional feelings are human and carnal in nature. The difference is between heaven and earth.

So do not attach much importance to your physical or emotional feelings, although they make you feel good and joyful or even ecstatic on occasion. Always put your faith to work first when you come to wait on the Lord. Just love the Lord with all your heart and soul and mind. Long to be in His presence. Cherish His presence. The more you long for and treasure the presence of God, the more He will manifest it in your heart and life—and in your meetings!

The Spirit of God often touches or fills us in a way that allows us to *feel* His presence, power, and sweetness in order to make us know that Jesus our risen Savior *is real and precious*! This God does for us individually as well as corporately to renew and strengthen our faith from time to time.

DEALING WITH WANDERING THOUGHTS

The other question that has often come up is how to deal with wandering thoughts. This is a common problem encountered by many Christians who have attempted the practice of waiting on God.

In the beginning of this practice, you will almost certainly find your thoughts flying around or your mind being bombarded with all kinds of bad and unwelcome thoughts. That is perfectly natural for the beginner. Even people who have practiced waiting on God for years still have unwanted thoughts. You will probably have a hard time trying to rein in your thoughts and keep them focused on Jesus. If this is the case, do not get fretful or frustrated. What matters is that you are in the presence of God as you wait on Him.

It is only natural when the body is inactive and trying to get quiet and still before God, that the mind is apt to "take off"; even when we are asleep, our mind remains active. This is why we dream during our sleep. But if you find your thoughts roaming when you wait on the Lord, you can always recall them and direct them toward Jesus. As you keep up the practice, the Spirit of God will help you and reward you in due time.

In the early stages of this practice, you will probably have to spend a great deal of time in training your mind to stay focused on Jesus. It will take time to discipline your mind, but if you persevere and believe that God is there to help you, you *will* succeed and see encouraging results before long. You will gradually find that not only can you focus on Jesus but also that the presence of God is so real and precious that you will want to spend more time waiting on the Lord. You will also find that the more you wait on the Lord, the more you will want to wait on Him.

The Power of Thinking (the Bible Way)

The Bible clearly teaches us what to think and how to think; what we think makes us who we are. "For as he [or she] thinks in his heart, so is he." (Proverbs 23:7aNKJV) This verse tells us something about the power of thinking! But thank God who "has not given us a spirit of fear [or negative mind], but of power and of love and of a sound mind." (1 Timothy 1:7NKJV) The Amplified Version has added these words: "but [He has given us a spirit] of calm and well-balanced mind and discipline and self-control."

As sons and daughters of God, we have been endued with what Jesus calls the "power from on high," i.e. supernatural power, power to forgive and to love, power to overcome temptations, and power to reject negative thoughts! Yes, we have power to discipline our mind and power for self-control and, as we keep up the practice of waiting on God, we will eventually be able to speak and think as the Bible teaches.

Set Your Mind on Things Above

The Bible commands us, "Set your hearts on things above [i.e. in heaven], where Christ is seated at the right hand of God. Set your minds on things above, not on earthly things." (Colossians 3:1-2) To set your mind on things above means to let Christ and the kingdom of God take hold of your heart and mind. In other words, God wants us to think more of Christ and less of earthly things. God wants all of us to be heavenly-minded people because "our citizenship is in heaven."

(Philippians 3:20) Above all, God wants to change us from within. God will do this for us when we take time to wait upon Him.

Today Christ is seated in heaven, but He also lives in our hearts; He is closer to us than we know. As we think of Christ more and read and meditate on His Word more, we will become more heavenly-minded while still living on the earth; we will become more like God's Son Jesus Christ. The Apostle Paul describes this process of transformation as "the renewing of your mind," adding, "Then you will be able to test and approve what God's will is—His good, pleasing and perfect will." (Romans 12:2b)

"Fix your thoughts on Jesus." (Hebrews 3:1b) We, as Christians, are instructed not only to think *more* of Jesus but also to have our thoughts *fixed* on Jesus—to think of Jesus at all times! We do not realize how little we think of Jesus in our everyday life. But the practice of waiting on God provides an excellent opportunity to learn to "fix our thoughts on Jesus"—to think about His wonderful teachings, His character, His love and compassion, His purity and humility, His absolute obedience and faithfulness to the Father, His sufferings, His crucifixion and resurrection. This is positive thinking, in the true sense of the word. This kind of thinking cannot but gradually change us into the likeness of Jesus Christ.

So whenever you find your thoughts wandering as you wait on the Lord, simply recall them and turn your heart to Jesus and give Him your loving attention. Just think of Jesus. Talk to Him both in your heart and aloud. Jesus is not far from you. He lives in your heart by His Spirit. We Christians should think and talk about the virtues of Jesus more, even when we are not waiting on the Lord. This would certainly help us to fix our thoughts on Jesus more easily.

"You will keep him in perfect peace whose mind is stayed on You." (Isaiah 26:3aNKJV) We all need to have peace of mind. We all want that perfect peace that Isaiah speaks of. Do we not? Then train your mind to stay on Jesus who is the Prince of Peace. As you keep at it, the Holy Spirit will help you succeed. Having your mind fixed on Jesus will slowly but surely bring you into that "perfect peace"—that divine, inner peace that comes from God.

Looking Unto Jesus

"Let us fix our eyes on Jesus, the author and perfecter of our faith." (Hebrews 12:2a) The King James Version renders it this way: "Looking unto Jesus, the author and finisher of our faith." In the original sense, the three words "looking unto Jesus" also have the connotation of "looking away from everything and everyone else save Jesus only"—the One who has conquered sin, the flesh, the world, the devil and death!

This is the kind of Savior we need to look up to—to have our eyes fixed upon Him at all times! There are times in our Christian life when we find ourselves in despair and helplessness. But we can always lift up our heads and look unto Jesus, "the author and perfecter of our faith," and presently, we will feel encouraged and uplifted with renewed hope!

So whenever you feel discouraged in your Christian walk, as the going gets tough, *look unto Jesus.* Do not look at your problems. Do not look at your circumstances. Do not look at the people around you. Do not look at the devil. Do not look at yourself. *Look at Jesus only.* This is the secret of victory. However difficult the situation, turn it over to Jesus, whatever the problem, leave it to Him. Jesus will not fail you. Jesus never fails! Nothing is impossible with God! Trust Him to work things out for your good because you love Him. "We know that all things work together for good to those who love God." (Romans 8:28a)

Holy Spirit: Our Helper and Teacher

Let me digress a little bit to interject a word about the crucial role of the Holy Spirit in our practice of waiting on God. For the practice to be meaningful and fruitful, we need to know the Holy Spirit who is God Himself—the third Person of the Godhead—and trust Him wholeheartedly to bring about the desired benefits and results.

The Bible tells us clearly that the Holy Spirit has been given to us as the all-powerful Helper and Teacher in all areas of our Christian life, especially in our relationship with God. Jesus says, "No one comes to the Father [God] except through me." In another instance, He says, "I am the vine; you are the branches. If a man remains in me and I in him, he will bear much fruit; apart from me you can do nothing." (John

14:6b, 15:5) If you read the context of the Lord's discourse, you will know that in both instances Jesus was talking about the Holy Spirit, who was to take His place after His physical departure from the scene. Jesus was saying, in effect, "No one comes to God except through the Holy Spirit; you need to live in the Spirit in order to bear much fruit, because apart from the Holy Spirit, you can do nothing."

Both the Lord Jesus and the Apostle John have told us specifically that the Holy Spirit who lives in us today has been sent to "teach us all things" and to "guide us into all truth." Jesus says, "The Holy Spirit, whom the Father will send in my name, will teach you all things...He will guide you into all truth." (John 14:26a, 16:13a) On the other hand, John used the term "anointing" to describe the role of the indwelling Spirit as our Teacher and Guide. He says, "The anointing you received from Him remains in you, and you do not need anyone to teach you. But as His anointing teaches you about all things, remain in Him." (1 John 2:27) Here, John tells us further that the Holy Spirit has come to dwell in us so that we may learn to live a life of abiding in Christ.

In the practice of waiting on God, we need to learn to be taught and led by God the Holy Spirit. If you come with an open mind and a humble and teachable spirit, the Holy Spirit will teach and guide you. If you learn to be led by the Holy Spirit in your practice of waiting on God, you will be led by the Spirit in other areas of your life as well. The Holy Spirit who is omniscient knows all about us; He knows our respective capacities, and He knows how to communicate to us at our varying levels. So as you take time to wait on the Lord, being eager and expectant to learn from the Holy Spirit, He will truly teach you in His own way—"a little here, a little there"—about everything you need to know concerning God's will for your life and for the church as a whole.

In the area of controlling your rambling thoughts as well as in the other aspects of waiting on God, you need to rely wholeheartedly on the Holy Spirit; *have faith* in Him, and believe with all your heart that He is there to do all that is necessary for you. Just trust in Him. Be conscious of Him as you wait on the Lord. "Now the Lord is the Spirit, and where the Spirit of the Lord is, there is freedom." (2 Corinthians 3:17) The Holy Spirit can and will bring your unwanted thoughts under control. He is able to do far more than you can ask or think.

As you continue to wait on the Lord, and learn to trust Him wholeheartedly, the Holy Spirit will enable you to even control your speech and actions, your temperament, and the evil desires of your heart. By the power of the Holy Spirit who dwells in you, you will be able to "take captive [or capture] every thought to make it obedient to Christ." (2 Corinthians 10:5b)

Recognizing the Presence of God

As I mentioned before, the practice of waiting on God is actually a practice of coming into—and eventually living in—the presence of God. But how do we recognize the presence of God? Someone asked, "How would you describe the presence of God?"

When we talk about the presence of God, we are not talking about heaven where Christ sits at the right hand of God; we are talking about something wonderful and glorious here on earth, something that every born-again and Spirit-filled Christian can know and experience.

What is the presence of God? It is a sense or an awareness of the invisible God or His Spirit being present with us inwardly or outwardly; it is a consciousness or realization of God being on the scene, oftentimes with awesomeness or a strong sense of soothing and gentle yet overwhelming power. Usually, it is just an atmosphere filled with indescribable peace, comfort, and pleasantness. This is due to the presence of the One who is the God of peace and comfort.

Oftentimes, the presence of God is absolute silence and quietness; a holy hush, if you will, where you can hear even the drop of a pin. Sometimes, as we get quiet and still before God, the presence of the Lord is so strong and engaging that we just want to sit still and remain silent and motionless, lest the sacred peace and tranquility should be disturbed. At other times, the presence of God is so rich and full that it permeates a room or an assembly hall, and the entire place becomes "holy ground." For where the presence of God is, there is holy ground, be it in a church sanctuary, a house, a room or a car.

The presence of God often brings a sense of great joy and excitement, or even an occasional ecstasy; someone has best described it as a "sense of ineffable glory," a result of the manifestation of the glorified Jesus. The Apostle Peter depicted it this way: "[Jesus Christ] whom having not seen you love. Though now you do not see Him, yet believing, you rejoice with joy inexpressible and full of glory." (1 Peter 1:8NKJV)

The greatest value of the practice of waiting on God is that it will slowly but surely usher us into the glorious presence of God. The presence of God is not just an experience; it is *God Himself.* If you know this truth, you will know that having the presence of God *means everything!*

There is something about the presence of God; the more you desire and cherish it, the more God will manifest it in your life. It is *the most important thing* in a Christian's life, particularly in the life and ministry of every servant of God. It is something so vital and indispensable that all Christians, particularly ministers of the Gospel, need to pray for and possess. Remember that our Lord Jesus said, "Apart from me, you can do nothing."

Moses, probably the greatest servant of God in Old Testament times, understood well what it means to have the presence of God. He had already witnessed some of the greatest and mightiest miracles performed by God as he led the people of Israel out of Egypt and in the wilderness. Yet he said to God: "If your Presence does not go with us, do not send us up [to the promised land]." God granted his request, saying, "My Presence will go with you, and I will give you rest." (Exodus 33:14,15) Peace and rest in the soul is the chief mark of the presence of God in a Christian's life. Love is, of course, another indication of the presence of God.

Manifestations of the Presence of God

Signs and wonders, like those recorded in the Book of Acts, are usually the most prominent manifestations of the presence and supernatural power of God. The presence of God, at varying times, also demonstrates divine wisdom, knowledge (not intellectual knowledge), spiritual authority, courage, meekness, purity, holiness, and righteousness.

Living in the presence of God does not necessarily mean that every day is exciting and glorious and that you no longer have any problems, but it does bring you a real sense of joy, peace and contentment, even in times of trials and affliction. It helps keep your priorities in order; it gives you a proper perspective of life, and of things that are of temporary value and those of eternal value. It takes away your fear and worry and fills your heart with hope and faith. It gives you a deep sense of satisfaction, confidence, and assurance, believing that since God is with you, all is well that ends well, no matter what happens to you.

There is something even more wonderful about the presence of God—it is this: It will make you humble, gentle, loving and kind. It will thoroughly change you—making you more like Jesus—if you live carefully in the presence of God. The practice of waiting on God will surely but gradually bring you into a life of living in God's presence.

We all know the story of Abraham. In spite of his early weaknesses, God appeared to him and said, "I am God Almighty; walk before me and be blameless." (Genesis 17:1) This short statement represents both a command and a promise. God was saying, in effect, to Abraham: "Walk before me and you will be perfect. I am God Almighty, and if you walk before me, I will make you perfect." Abraham did become perfect in faith and obedience.

So living carefully in the presence of God will make us like Abraham, the man of God and exemplary man of faith and obedience—and ultimately like Jesus Christ.

Recognizing the Voice of God

Jesus says, "I am the good shepherd; I know my sheep and my sheep know me…they too will listen to my voice." (John 10:14,16c) Every Christian knows Jesus as his/her personal Savior. But do you know Jesus as your personal Shepherd—the One who calls His sheep and leads, guides and feeds them? As His sheep, do you recognize your Shepherd's voice—the voice of His Holy Spirit?

One of the most important lessons to be learned, as we come to wait on the Lord, is to listen to His voice. When you wait upon the Lord, you need to be mindful that you have come into the presence of a living God who speaks to His people, and that He expects you to listen to His voice and obey it.

"In the past," the author of Hebrews writes at the outset, "God spoke to our forefathers through the prophets at many times and in various ways, but in these last days He has spoken to us by His Son." (Hebrews 1:1) We now live in the last days, the Spirit of God has spoken to us, and He still speaks to us. The question is: How many of us have heard

God's voice, that still small voice of the Holy Spirit? Of those who have heard the voice of God, how many have obeyed it?

As God is pouring out His Spirit upon the earth in these last days, He speaks to His people in various ways—in dreams, visions, prophecies, etc. God also speaks to us by means of divine revelation, inspiration, impression, and by the prompting of the Holy Spirit. God also speaks to us through His anointed faithful servants. Above all, God speaks to us by His inspired Word the Bible.

"But in these last days," as the Scripture says, "He has spoken to us by His Son"—the eternal Word that became flesh and is now the living Word of God. I, for one, believe that God speaks to us today primarily through His Word the Bible—inspired and enlightened by the Spirit of God. This is probably the most sensible and safest way of hearing God speak. (See section on "The Voice of God in the Bible")

Nevertheless, we should be mindful that the words we read in the Bible are merely literal words; unless they are *inspired* and *quickened* by the Holy Spirit, the words in themselves are lifeless and powerless. Words are useful only for information and instruction, but when the words in the Bible are *inspired* and *quickened* by the Spirit of God, they bring life and power, as the Apostle Paul points out, "for the letter kills, but the Spirit gives life." (2 Corinthians 3:6c)

"For the word of God is living and powerful, and sharper than any two-edged sword, piercing even to the division of soul and spirit, and of joints and marrow, and is a discerner of the thoughts and intents of the heart." (Hebrews 4:12NKJV) The Bible which is the written Word of God, or any part thereof, for that matter, becomes the "living and powerful" Word of God only when it is *inspired, anointed and made alive* by the Spirit of God.

So what we need is not just the Word, but the Spirit as well, so that the life-giving Spirit might breathe upon the words we read in the Bible; only then the words become "living and powerful" in a way that transforms our lives. The Holy Spirit, whom Jesus calls the Spirit of truth, has come to "guide you into all truth"—to make the Bible alive, meaningful and powerful! Indeed there is life and power in the Word of God!

But how do we recognize the voice of God? We recall how the prophet Elijah heard the voice of God on Mount Horeb, "the mountain of God." Elijah did not hear the voice of God in the mighty wind, earthquake and fire that took place at the time because God was not in them. It was only after these phenomena that Elijah heard "a gentle whisper" [or "a still small voice" as in KJV]. (1 Kings 19:11-13) That was the voice of God that Elijah had heard.

Job, another man of God, after describing the mighty works of God, had this to say of the voice of God: "How *faint* the whisper we hear of Him!" (Job 26:14b) Both of these godly men described the voice of God as a "whisper" or a "still small voice," yet "how *faint* the whisper!" Was it an audible voice that Elijah and Job had heard? I suppose not.

How then do we recognize the voice of God? In order to hear God speak, you need to go beyond the physical realm of your senses. Since God is the Spirit, the voice of God is the voice of the Holy Spirit. The Holy Spirit, being so loving and gentle, almost always speaks to us with a still, small, soft and tender voice, as a whisper too faint to be heard; it is usually an inaudible voice.

In order to hear the voice of God who is the Spirit, you need to be filled with the Spirit and learn to walk in the Spirit. You need to relate to the Holy Spirit. You need to be spiritually sensitive and alert. You need to be conscious of the Holy Spirit who dwells in you. You need to be in tune with God. You need to pay more attention to God. You need to get close to God—close enough to hear His voice. That is why we need the practice of waiting on God.

You also need to pray that God will give you the "hearing ear and the seeing eye" so you can hear God's inaudible voice and see His invisible face. "The hearing ear and the seeing eye, the Lord has made them both." (Proverbs 20:12NKJV) These are very special spiritual gifts; only the Lord can give them. Waiting on the Lord will allow Him to instill these gifts within us so that we may have the supernatural ability to hear God's voice and see God move in human affairs. How we need to hear God speak to us and see Jesus in our lives all the time!

Martha W. Robinson, a rare teacher on inner life in modern times, once said, "Seeing Jesus in meetings means seeing Him *all the time* outside of meetings." (For a sampling of Mrs. Robinson's teachings on Christian inward life, see Appendixes 1 and 2. For the complete story of her life and ministry, read "Radiant Glory" by Gordon P. Gardiner, published by BREAD OF LIFE, 445 Harman Street, Brooklyn, N. Y. 11237)

For those of you who believe in prophecies, visions, dreams, tongues and interpretation of tongues, it is necessary that these be examined and confirmed in light of the Scriptures and external circumstances. Regarding circumstantial confirmation, we have the Biblical example of Gideon who sought external confirmation of what God had said to him by putting out the fleece not only once but twice, and God confirmed His word. (Judges 6:36-40). Remember, *the voice of God never runs contrary to the Word of God.*

The Bible teaches that we are not to "treat prophecies [or for that matter, any of those things mentioned in the Bible] with contempt" but "test *everything.* Hold on to the good. Avoid every kind of evil." (1 Thessalonians 5:20-22)

THE VOICE OF GOD IN THE BIBLE

You might ask, "How do I know if God is speaking to me when I am reading my Bible?" Well, you can tell it in several ways: When you are moved—sometimes even to tears—by what you read; or you are so touched by what you read that you start crying out aloud. These are certain indications of the Holy Spirit speaking to your heart!

The words you read suddenly appear "larger" or seem to have "jumped out" of the page; or the words you read suddenly take on new meaning. These are also indications that God *is* speaking to you.

There are times when God "drops" a word or two in your heart, and you are not sure if it is from God. There are several ways to ascertain its source:

If it is a word straight from the Bible;
If it immediately lifts you up;
If it encourages and comforts you;
If it lightens or takes away your burden;
If it enlightens you as to certain spiritual truth;
If it removes your doubts;
If it strengthens your faith and gives you new hope;
If it sets you free from a certain bondage;
If you clearly sense the anointing of the Holy Spirit;
Above all, if it brings you closer to Jesus and makes you love Him more.

If your answer to these "ifs" is positive, then you can be sure that it is the voice of God.

Sometimes you read a passage or chapter in the morning and you do not feel anything while reading it. Then later on during the day, somebody inadvertently brings up something that you remember having read in that particular passage or chapter. If this happens, it means that you probably missed hearing God in the morning, and that He *is* talking to you again!

Sometimes the Holy Spirit Himself will remind you of something you have read in the Bible previously; now He is speaking to you again. Yes, we do often miss hearing the Lord due to our carelessness, spiritual dullness and insensitivity. We need to pray for greater sensitivity as much as we need to pray for more wisdom, love and faith.

Sometimes a passage or verse that you have read repeatedly which never seemed to make sense becomes meaningful and powerful to you all at once! This is another indication of the Holy Spirit speaking to you.

Usually, God does not get our attention easily, but if we are sensitive to the Holy Spirit and alert to what God may have to say to us when we read the Bible, we will hear the voice of God.

The Spirit of Humility and Poverty

Finally, it is of utmost importance that we come into the presence of God with a spirit of humility and poverty, recognizing that we are but sinners saved by grace—that are nothing, have nothing, and can do nothing without Him. This humble attitude is absolutely essential to the success and fruitfulness of the practice of waiting on God.

Conversely, if we come to wait on God our Creator with a know-it-all attitude, we will never receive anything from Him. For "God opposes the proud, but gives grace to the humble." (James 4:6b; 1 Peter 5:5c)

Humility is the basic condition to receive favor and grace from God. Humility is of Christ while pride is of the devil. That is why God is against the proud and arrogant but favors the humble and poor in spirit.

"For thus says the High and Lofty One who inhabits eternity, whose name is Holy: 'I dwell in the high and holy place, with him who has a contrite and humble spirit, to revive the spirit of the humble, and to revive the heart of the contrite ones.'" (Isaiah 57:15NKJV) If we come to wait on God with a humble and broken spirit, He will surely revive our hearts, bless us and dwell with us—the Most High God dwelling with the humble man/woman—as He has promised.

Jesus says, "Blessed are the poor in spirit, for theirs is the kingdom of God. Blessed are the meek [or humble], for they will inherit the earth." (Matthew 5:3,5) Here the kingdom of God and the earth both represent the richness and fullness of God. If we come to wait on God with a spirit of humility and poverty, God will surely bless us and reveal to us "the unsearchable riches of Christ," as He did for the Apostle Paul. (Ephesians 3:8)

As we wait on the Lord, we should pray that God will grant us that blessed spirit of humility and poverty so that we may find favor with Him. We should pray that God will grant us a *teachable* spirit as well as a spirit of obedience. These are some of the essential ingredients of humility; a humble person is always obedient, but a humble person with a *teachable* spirit is not only obedient, but also quick to learn and readily receptive to the teachings of our Lord who is the Holy Spirit.

Humility is a gift of God; it is not found in the natural man/woman. Humility is not just a Christian virtue or one of the characteristics of Christ; it is *Christ Himself.*

> *"Your attitude should be the same as that of Christ Jesus Who, being in very nature God, did not consider equality with God something to be grasped, but made Himself nothing, taking the very nature of a servant, being made in human likeness, and being found in appearance as a man, He humbled Himself and became obedient to death—even death on a cross!"* (Philippians 2:5-8)

Chapter Five

THE BENEFITS OF WAITING ON GOD

✠ ✠ ✠

THE BIBLE IS REPLETE WITH GOD'S PROMISES that if we draw near to God, He will reward us and bless us beyond our expectation. If we truly know that our God is the One "from whom all blessings flow," we will not fail to come to wait on Him, and God will not fail to meet our needs. "For no matter how many promises God has made, they are 'Yes' in Christ." (2 Corinthians 1:20a)

Among God's promises are these simple but profound truths: "In returning [to me] and rest [in me] you shall be saved. In quietness and confidence shall be your strength. But you would not....Therefore, the Lord will wait that He may be gracious to you....Those who wait on the Lord shall renew their strength. They shall mount up with wings like eagles, they shall run and not be weary, they shall walk and not faint." (Isaiah 30:15,18a; 40:31NKJV)

Jesus has unequivocally promised, "Come to me, all you who are weary and burdened, and I will give you rest. Take my yoke upon you and learn from me, for I am gentle and humble in heart, and you will find rest for your souls." (Matthew 11:28-29) This promise is not just for sinners; it is for all who are weary and burdened, perhaps especially for those ministers and church leaders who find their work for the Lord increasingly stressful and burdensome.

The Benefits of Waiting on God Are Innumerable

The benefits to be reaped from the practice of waiting on God are innumerable. To mention only a few:

1. It will develop and enhance your personal relationship with God.
2. It will increase your personal knowledge of God.
3. It will bring you into real intimacy with God.
4. It will enrich your spiritual life and cause you to go deeper in God.
5. It will usher you into a growing sense of the presence of God.
6. It will lead you into a life of abiding in Christ.
7. It will bring you inner peace, rest and joy.
8. It will make you increasingly sensitive to the Holy Spirit.
9. It will enable you to recognize and overcome your carnality.
10. It will make you want Jesus more and long to be more like Him.

Amazingly enough, as you get quiet and come down before the Lord, allowing Him the opportunity and freedom to do what He desires for you, the Spirit of God will bring about the above-mentioned benefits. As you persist in the practice of waiting on God, He will do much more for you—above all you ask or think. For the Bible says, "He rewards those who earnestly seek Him." (Hebrews 11:6c)

Gerhard Tersteegen, an eighteenth century German "mystic" who knew well the secret of waiting on God in silence, is said to have made this profound statement: "Miracles are often wrought by God within those who wait on Him in silence." Waiting on God in silence will do for you what external activities cannot do—bring you deeper into God, and eventually into a wonderful union with God!

One of the reasons for the lack of real spirituality and depth in Christianity today is perhaps due to the fact that Christians by and large are not taught the incredible value of waiting on the Lord—spending time alone with God in private. "Very few of us," said A. W. Tozer, "are ever really alone with God." No wonder there is so much outwardness and shallowness in Christianity today.

Many church-going Christians seem to be satisfied with the status quo, not knowing that God has much more in store for them and that we can grow deeper and become richer and happier as Christians. There are so many people in the world who want to know about how to get rich financially, but very few people, even among Christians, ever really care about becoming rich spiritually.

Jesus warns, "Watch out! Be on your guard against all kinds of greed; a man's life does not consist in the abundance of his possessions" but in being "rich toward God." He asks, "What good will it be for a man if he gains the whole world, yet forfeits his soul? Or what can a man give in exchange for his soul?" (Luke 12:15,21; Matthew 16:26)

Greed—this inherently insatiable desire for more—and other excessive desires of the human heart and flesh preclude a Christian from seeking what the Apostle Paul describes as "the unsearchable riches of Christ." But the practice of waiting on God in a consistent manner will make us eternally rich—yes, rich forever—in the Lord!

To be eternally rich, you will have to find Christ for yourself. You must not be satisfied with mere religion or religious practices. There must be that personal encounter and fellowship with God. You must be sure that you have—i.e. knowingly possess—Jesus Christ, and that Christ is in you and you are in Him. "For in Him dwells all the fullness of the Godhead bodily; and you are complete in Him." (Colossians 2:9,10aNKJV) A paraphrased translation of this richly revealing verse makes the original more plain and meaningful: "So you have everything when you have Christ, and you are filled with God through your union with Christ." (Living Letters: The Paraphrased Epistles—Kenneth N. Taylor).

Christianity is not just a religion; it is a personal relationship with the living Christ. It is a mystic union with Christ wrought by the Holy Spirit so that we may share "all the fullness of the Godhead" that is in Christ.

True Christianity is Christ living in the believer! The person who believes in Christianity is called a *Christian* simply because he/she has Christ living in him/her. The practice of waiting on God, if carried out on a regular basis, will surely and increasingly bring Christ in and drive so-called religion out! But this kind of work can be accomplished by none other than the Spirit of God Himself, who will do wonders for us as we take time to wait upon Him.

Benefits Enumerated and Elaborated

Let me go on to outline some of the most important areas of our Christian lives in which we can confidently expect to benefit from the practice of waiting on God:

1. *Personal relationship with God:* This is the most important thing in a Christian's life, i.e. to know God in a personal and experiential way. After all, Christianity is a personal and practical religion. As Christians, we must be born again and, better yet, filled with the Holy Spirit, and have a living personal relationship with God as His children. The practice of waiting on God will certainly help develop and enhance our personal relationship with God.
2. *Personal knowledge of God:* Generally speaking, there are two ways in which Christians can know God: one is intellectual—i.e. knowledge gained by reading the Bible and religious books; and the other is spiritual or inspirational—i.e. knowledge that comes directly from God the Spirit. The former is in the head, the latter in the heart, often referred to as "head knowledge" and "heart knowledge." Although the head and the heart are only a little more than a foot apart distance-wise, the difference between head knowledge and heart knhowledge in knowing God is huge—as great as between heaven and earth; so we must seek to know God not just in the head but in the heart as well. Waiting on the Lord will provide an excellent opportunity to gain a personal and intimate knowledge of God.
3. *Intimacy with God:* Since waiting on God is a way of drawing near to Him, prolonged practice will undoubtedly develop intimacy with our beloved Savior. We will find Jesus increasingly real and precious in our hearts and souls, and that our desire and love for Him will grow as our relationship with God deepens. Again, this is the work of the Holy Spirit who has come to guide

us into a relationship as intimate as the one described between the Beloved and His Bride in the Song of Songs.

4. *The presence of God:* The practice of waiting on God is one of the most effective ways of entering into the presence of the Lord. Waiting on God actually means coming into as well as remaining in the presence of God; it is a beginning of the process of developing a deeper and lasting sense of the presence of God in a Christian's life. Waiting on God will make you increasingly conscious of God's presence so that eventually you will find yourself living in the presence of God day in and day out. Consequently, the chorus that begins with this wonderful sentence, "It is glory just to walk with Him," will become a reality in your walk with God. There is much more about the presence of God that you will have to discover for yourself as you spend time waiting on the Lord!
5. *Abiding in Christ:* Many Christians are familiar with the parable of the vine and its branches that Jesus used to teach us about our union with and dependence upon Him. But few of us have sought—much less attained—a life of abiding in Christ. Constantly abiding in Christ is the secret of fruitfulness and victory over every area of our Christian life! We may have the doctrine of Christ, but do we have the reality of Christ living in us and of our abiding in Him? The practice of waiting on God, however, will pave the way of entering into not only the presence of God but also a joyful and victorious life of abiding in Christ.
6. *Spiritual wealth and depth:* Waiting on the Lord will certainly enrich your spiritual life and experience as your knowledge of God increases and deepens. Although spiritual wealth and depth are rare commodities in modern Christianity, they can be developed over time by the daily practice of waiting on God, the in-depth study of the Word of God, and constant fellowship with Jesus. A true sense of richness and contentment resulting from a growing knowledge of God will eventually emerge as you take time to wait upon the Lord.

7. *Inner peace, joy and rest:* These divine gifts are specifically promised as our relationship with God grows closer and deeper—as we become increasingly united to the One who is "the God of peace" and "the Lord of the Sabbath." How we need the peace of God and the joy of the Lord! God has promised a divine rest for all His children. God will bring those who take time to wait upon Him into His divine peace and rest. Once we are brought into this blessed state of peace, joy, and rest, these gifts become ours as long as we remain connected to the Lord who is the Source of all our supply; they become part and parcel of our spiritual inheritance.
8. *Spiritual sensitivity and discernment:* These are among the most important qualities to be possessed by any Christian. Again these qualities are obtained only from God and developed by Him as we draw near to the One who is the Giver of every good and perfect gift. Spiritual sensitivity comes from yielding to the Holy Spirit; the more we are led by the Holy Spirit, the more we will become spiritually sensitive. Meanwhile, discernment is probably the most important of all spiritual gifts; the Bible calls it "discerning of spirits," without which one can hardly distinguish between "the Spirit of truth and the spirit of falsehood"—i.e. between what is of Christ and what is of the anti-Christ. (1 John 4:3,6)
9. *Recognizing and overcoming the flesh:* Interestingly, as we become more sensitive to the Holy Spirit, we also become more sensitive to the flesh—or our own ego—because the two are against each other. The Holy Spirit not only gives us the ability to recognize the flesh but also the power to overcome it. Waiting on the Lord—i.e. to be united to the One who has conquered the flesh, the world, sin and the devil—is the process whereby we are gradually sensitized to the flesh and continually empowered to overcome it.
10. *Greater hunger and thirst for Jesus Himself:* The most important single lesson to be learned in the practice of waiting on God is to be focused on Jesus alone. As Jesus becomes the center and substance of our waiting on God, we begin to enjoy our fellowship with Him in silent prayer, worship and praise,

singing from the heart, and even dancing in the Spirit. Our communion with Jesus becomes sweeter and His love grows increasingly palatable and satisfying. We begin to appreciate the wonder of Jesus Himself! We discover that Jesus is all we need to satisfy our hearts and souls and that He meets all our needs! As we become enamored of Jesus, our desire and love for just Jesus Himself also grow intensely. There is also more hunger for the Word of God. Strangely, the more we come to know Jesus, the more we want to know Him; the more we discover His great love for us, the more we want to love Him! It is just that wonderful!

All of these spiritual benefits—and much more—will be yours if you invest your precious time in this practice of waiting on the Lord who "longs to be gracious to you....Blessed are all who wait for Him." (Isaiah 30:18)

PHYSICAL EXERCISE VERSUS SPIRITUAL EXERCISE

The Bible says, "Physical training is of some value, but godliness [i.e. godly spiritual exercise] has value for all things, holding promise for both the present life and the life to come." (1 Timothy 4:8) For this reason, the Apostle Paul urged the young man Timothy, "Train yourself to be godly." This is what waiting on God is all about—to train oneself to be godly, i.e. Christlike.

Many people spend their time and money on physical fitness and health care while neglecting the state of their souls and hearts, the soundness of which can be sustained only by constant spiritual exercise—the godly practice of waiting on God.

While physical exercise has "some value" and is good for our present life, godly exercise has "value for all things" and is good not only for this life but also for the life to come. And it is free of charge! The only price required is some of your time. In the secular world, time means money; in the spiritual world, time means more than money—it means life eternal, if it is spent wisely!

In addition to the numerous benefits of waiting on God as outlined above, there are at least four major areas where we can most assuredly expect to benefit from the practice of waiting upon the Lord. For these are the promises as well as the purposes of God which will be fulfilled by none other than God Himself as we allow Him to work freely on our behalf.

Gaining New Strength and Power

The prophet Isaiah, who knew the secret of waiting upon the Lord, writes, "Have you not known? Have you not heard? The everlasting God, the Creator of the ends of the earth…He gives power to the weak, and to those who have no might He increases strength…Those who wait on the Lord shall renew their strength." (Isaiah 40:28-29,31aNKJV)

Read the entire fortieth chapter of the Book of Isaiah, and you will understand why "those who wait on the Lord shall renew their [or find new] strength."

Dear brother or sister, are you wearied? Are you tired of trying to be a good Christian? Are you still struggling with your weaknesses? Are you being stressed out on your job or in your ministry? Do you not know that our God, the Creator of heavens and the earth, "gives power to the weak" and strength to the weary? Have you not heard that "those who wait on the Lord shall renew their strength"?

Isaiah further writes, "Even the youths shall faint and be weary, and the young men shall utterly fall. But those who wait on the Lord shall renew their strength; they shall mount up with wings like eagles, they shall run and not be weary, they shall walk and not faint."

God is saying to us, in effect, through the prophet, "No matter how strong and intelligent you may think you are, the day will come when you find yourself powerless and helpless; you have come to the end of your rope, and you are ready to give up." Sometimes we hear people say, "I can't take it anymore!" Is that where you are now? Do not give up! Help is on the way!

"But"—notice what God says in His Word and I am paraphrasing it—"But those who wait on the Lord will always find new strength; they will be able to live over and above the dark clouds and storms, they will always have sunshine in their hearts, and they will never be tired or worn out." It took me many years to discover this wonderful truth!

Dear Christian, have you not heard our loving Savior calling? Here is His long- standing invitation to you: "Come to me, all you who are weary and burdened, and I will give you rest. Take my yoke upon you [i.e. being connected to Him] and learn from me, for I am gentle and humble in heart, and you will find rest for your souls. For my yoke is easy and my burden is light." (Matthew 11:28-30)

Being Transformed Into the Image of Jesus

One of the most amazing results from the practice of waiting on God is the natural but gradual transformation of our old life into the likeness of Jesus Christ. The change, for the most part, comes slowly but surely as we continue to wait on the Lord. This is the wonderful work of the Spirit of God within us in ways beyond our comprehension.

God in His plan of salvation has predetermined that we as sinners should be not only saved from eternal damnation but also transformed into the image of His Son Jesus Christ. "And we know that in all things God works for the good of those who love Him, who have been called according to His purpose. For those God foreknew He also predestined to be conformed to the likeness of His Son, that He might be the firstborn among many brothers." (Romans 8:28-29)

The practice of waiting on God provides the best opportunity for God to bring about this glorious change in our lives. We can never change ourselves. Since God has made us, He alone can change us. We are "predestined" to be changed. We are bound to change as long as we continue to spend time waiting upon the Lord. God effects this change by the life-changing power of His Holy Spirit working within us as we remain quiet and reverent before Him, reading and meditating on His Word and communing with Him.

The Bible speaks of "putting off the old man" and "putting on the new man." This is an inner evolution from our sinful human nature to the sinless divine nature of Christ, being made "partakers of the divine nature." (Ephesians 4:22,24; Colossians 3:9-10; 2 Peter 1:3-4) God in His redemptive plan has predestined us to be changed into the likeness of His Son Jesus Christ, and we *will* be changed as we obey the Word of God and follow the leading of the Holy Spirit.

Another way, perhaps a harsh way, for God to change us is by His discipline or chastisement. He may put us through hot waters or bring some type of affliction until we are willing to change our own ways and are ready to be corrected. For those who stand ready to obey God's Word and follow the leading of His Holy Spirit, God will not have to resort to these harsh measures in order to soften our hearts and change our attitudes. "For He does not willingly bring affliction or grief to the children of men." (Lamentations 3:33)

The easiest and painless way for God to change us—and change we must—is when we spend lots of time waiting on the Lord and studying His Word. More importantly, we need to obey the commandments in God's Word in our daily life. Obedience is the key to the fulfillment of God's purposes in our lives.

Meanwhile, any noticeable change in our lives is an indication of our spiritual growth. How do we know whether we have advanced spiritually? Not by judging whether we have studied the Bible everyday and attended church regularly, but by the actual changes others see in our attitudes, behavior, feelings, words and actions. Unless we have shown these changes, we should never be satisfied with our spiritual condition because we have not grown in the Lord.

In God's sight, it does not matter how much we know the Bible, how much we pray, or how frequently we go to church. These religious practices would be totally meaningless unless we are changed from glory to glory—i.e. becoming increasingly like Jesus Christ. All that matters to God is this: Are we more like Jesus today than yesterday? Have we become more loving, kind and humble? Otherwise, we have not grown, we are not in God's eternal plan, and we are not part of that Holy City called New Jerusalem. We cannot be counted as the Bride of the Lamb.

Nevertheless, if we keep up the practice of waiting on God as suggested in this book, God will certainly change us and make us more and more like His Son Jesus Christ. God will bring about that marvelous transformation by the wonder-working power of His Holy Spirit as we spend more time in His presence, gazing upon His beauty and glory.

> *"But we all, with unveiled face, beholding as in a mirror the glory of the Lord, are being transformed into the same image from glory to glory, just as by the Spirit of the Lord."* (2 Corinthians 3:18NKJV)

Union with God

In these last days, we are hearing more talk about intimacy with God. Many Christians are seeking an intimate relationship with God. Why? Because this is a sign that Jesus is coming back soon, probably sooner than we expect, and the Holy Spirit is working urgently to prepare the church as the Bride of Christ. Those who consider themselves the Bride-to-be waiting for "the wedding of the Lamb" must be prepared—i.e. changed into His image from glory to glory—for His imminent return!

From the Biblical perspective, the terminology "Bride of Christ" means being united to the Lamb of God in all His virtues—His love, righteousness, selflessness, holiness, purity, humility, obedience and gentleness. In short, it means that we are transformed into the likeness of Jesus Christ—fit to be His Bride, as the Bible describes, "prepared as a bride beautifully dressed for her husband." (Revelation 21:2b)

We need to seek intimacy with God, but we also need to seek union with God—to be more deeply united with Christ who is our coming Bridegroom. It is for this ultimate and highest purpose that God is pouring out His Spirit copiously in these last days so that the Church of Christ may be fully prepared as His Bride.

The idea of union between God and man—a topic rarely discussed these days—has been in God's heart since the beginning of human history. The symbolic significance of this divine union was reflected in the world's first marriage between Adam and Eve as instituted and ordained by God Himself. "For this reason," the Scripture says, "a man will leave his father and mother and be united to his wife, and they will become one flesh [or body]." (Genesis 2:24)

When Jesus was asked about the issue of divorce, He referred to this same verse, and added, "They [the husband and wife] are no longer two, but one. Therefore what God has joined together, let man not separate." (Matthew 19:6) The reason that Jesus ruled out divorce, except in case of adultery, is that marriage between a man and a woman represents something sacred and dear to the heart of God, the One who initiated the time-honored institution; it is a symbol of holy union between God the Creator and man the creature.

The symbolic meaning of marriage between a man and a woman was further made clear by the Apostle Paul as he taught about the relationship between husbands and wives. He counsels, "Wives, submit to your own husbands, as to the Lord…Husbands, love your wives, just as Christ also loved the church and gave Himself for her…For we are members of His body, of His flesh and of His bones." (Ephesians 5:22,23NKJV)

Paul made it unequivocally clear that we as born-again Christians are so united to Christ that "we are members of His body, of His flesh and of His bones." He also quoted the same verse from Genesis: "For this reason, a man shall leave his father and mother and be joined to his wife, and the two shall become one flesh." Then he added, "This is a great mystery, but I speak concerning Christ and the church"—meaning he was talking about the union between Christ and the church. (Ephesians 5:31-32NKJV)

This union with God, a much deeper Christian experience, is also clearly taught by our Lord Jesus when He spoke about the significance of Pentecost—about the ministry of the Holy Spirit—in Chapters 14, 15 and 16 according to the Gospel of John.

"On that day," said Jesus, "you will realize that I am in my Father, and you are in me, and I am in you." This wonderful union with the Holy Trinity is made possible through the ministry of the Holy Spirit or, as some would call it, "the baptism of the Holy Spirit"; it is the deeper work of the Holy Spirit that dwells within us, a work that can be accomplished more easily and effectively as we wait on the Lord *in silence* perhaps than in any other way.

When we talk about the baptism of the Holy Spirit here, we are not just talking about signs and wonders, dreams and visions, or the gifts of the Spirit; we are talking about a deepening and uniting relationship with God—the union between God and man—the reason why Jesus the Son of God baptizes with the Holy Spirit. (John 1:32-34)

"On that day," Jesus said, meaning the day when you are baptized or filled with the Holy Spirit, and furthermore, indwelled and ruled by the Holy Spirit, "you will realize that I am in my Father, and you are in me, and I am in you." This is the supreme significance of Pentecost—the Holy Spirit has come to unite us to God the Father, God the Son and, of course, God the Spirit. God dwells in man and man in God—"This is a great mystery!"

We see clearly in Jesus the embodiment—the perfect model—of this wonderful union between God and man. Although Jesus—the man in God and God in him—walked and taught in their midst for over three years, yet the disciples failed to recognize him as such.

"Don't you know me," Jesus said to Philip who asked Him to show them the Father, "even after I have been among you such a long time? Anyone who has seen me has seen the Father. Don't you believe that I am in the Father, and that the Father is in me? Believe me when I say that I am in the Father and the Father is in me." (John 14:9-11)

Then Jesus went on to explain how this union between God and man could become a fact of life: "I will ask the Father, and He will give you another Counselor to be with you forever—the Spirit of truth. The world cannot accept Him, because it neither sees Him nor knows Him. But you know Him, for He lives with you and will be [or is] in you...On that day you will realize that I am in my Father, and you are in me, and I am in you." (John 14:16-20)

Jesus came not only to deliver us from sin but, more significantly, to show us how we *can* live in God and God in us, whereby the man or woman with a sinful nature might be free from sin and the power of darkness. As Norman Harrison, a Plymouth Brethren devotional writer, put it: "Jesus walked this earth to show what God is like when He lives in a man, and what man is like when God lives in him."

Because Jesus the man lived in God and God in him, though he was "tempted in every way, just as we are," yet he was "without sin." If you live in God and God in you, you cannot live in sin, as the Apostle John says, "No one who lives in Him keeps on sinning." (Hebrews 4:15b; 1 John 3:6a)

Jesus came not only to show us the way of being united with God, He has also made this union possible through the baptism and indwelling of the Holy Spirit. As we take time to wait on the Lord faithfully and patiently, we will be giving God the opportunity and time to work out this profound truth in our lives.

The Holy Spirit Himself will, in time, bring about this wonderful union between God and us. For it is for this purpose that we are created and, by the same token, it is for this noble reason that the Holy Spirit has been given to us.

Knowing and Fulfilling the Will of God

One of the most important things in every Christian's life is knowing and doing the will of God. If you do not know the will of God for your life, you are in darkness, and you do not know where you are going. On the other hand, if you know and live in the will of God, you will realize that your life on earth has a meaningful purpose, is full of joy and happiness, and that you have a sense of fulfillment. One of the greatest benefits from the practice of waiting on God is that it helps us to know the will of God and enables us to walk in the will of God.

The Lord Jesus has warned long ago, "Not everyone who says to me, 'Lord, Lord,' will enter the kingdom of heaven, but only he who does the will of my Father who is in heaven. Many will say to me on that day [the Day of Judgment], 'Lord, Lord, did we not prophesy in your name, and in your name drive out demons and perform many miracles?' Then I will tell them plainly, 'I never knew you. Away from me, you evildoers!'" (Matthew 7:21-23)

"Not everyone who says to me, 'Lord, Lord,'"—this means obviously that not every nominal church-going Christian will enter the kingdom of heaven. Those who did those wonderful things in the name of the Lord—Jesus says there will be many of them—apparently represent the so-called ministers, preachers and evangelists, the ones who failed to do the will of God. The Lord says plainly that not only they will not enter the kingdom of heaven, but also they will be treated as "evildoers." This is all because they neither knew nor did the will of God.

We Christians have all too often taken things for granted. We think that as long as we study the Bible, pray and go to church regularly, and even get involved in some kind of ministry, we will be accepted into the kingdom of God, regardless of the will of God. This is not so, according to our Lord Jesus. He says, "only he [or she] who does the will of my Father" will enter the kingdom of heaven.

"Wake up, O sleeper," the Apostle Paul admonishes, "rise from the [spiritually] dead, and Christ will shine on you!" "Therefore," he goes on to say, "do not be foolish [unwise or ignorant of God's will], but understand what the Lord's will is." (Ephesians 5:14,17) One of the benefits from the practice of waiting on God is that Christ will shine on us—to enlighten us as to God's will for the church as well as for us individually.

Christians by and large tend to be preoccupied with the things of the world, such as success, prosperity and materialism. Greed seems to be a common sin among Christians and non-Christians alike. People always seem to want more of the things of the world, hardly the things of God. We do not seem to take to heart the Biblical teachings such as this: "Do not love the world or anything in the world. If anyone loves the world, the love of the Father is not in him. The world and its desires pass away, but the man [or woman] who does the will of God lives forever." (1 John 2:15,17)

Only the men and women who know and do the will of God will live forever—they will enter the kingdom of heaven. But how do we know the will of God? The question is often raised by God-seeking Christians. The best way to find out the will of God is, of course, by coming to God Himself and to His Word—to wait on the Lord and dig into the Word. The will of God is spelled out clearly in the Word of God the Bible, but much is yet to be revealed by the Holy Spirit.

We need to learn to avail ourselves of the access to the presence of God; we need to be immersed in His Word and expect His Holy Spirit to unveil the hidden meanings therein. This means that we need to spend more time alone with God. As we do so, God will give us the spiritual understanding we need of His will. He will also give us the power to obey His will. For God is eager to make His perfect will known to us because it is His pleasure that we know and walk in His will.

Once we come to understand that "good, pleasing and perfect will" of God, we will no longer want to have our own ways, we will readily embrace God's will, and we would love to do God's will.

In this regard, one of the best prayers I have heard is this: "Lord, make me to know your will, to love your will, and to do your will." If you would come to wait on God with this prayer request, you can be certain that God will make known His will to you and that He will enable you to do it.

Besides the Lord Jesus, the only man in the Bible whom God has called "a man after my own heart" is David. The reason that God replaced Saul with David as the King of Israel is simple. God said, "I have found David, a man after My own heart, who will do all My will." Obviously, God called David "a man after my own heart" not because he was perfect but because he wanted to do all God's will. Indeed, before he died, David "served his own generation by the will of God." (Acts 13:22b,36aNKJV)

As for God's will for our individual lives respectively, apart from that which is set forth in the Scriptures, this is a matter of how each one is to be led and guided by the Holy Spirit. For the benefit of those who sincerely desire to walk in the Spirit, I would venture to offer four guiding principles based upon years of my own experience of being led by the Holy Spirit. These principles are:

1. Do not make any move unless or until you have heard from the Lord—a word or two preferably from the Bible or some other means used by God. But you must first put aside your own pre-conceived ideas, desires and plans. You must be so single-minded that you want only God's will for your life, regardless of the cost.
2. There needs to be a consistent prompting or nagging of the Holy Spirit within, sometimes to the point of uneasiness and restlessness until the issue is addressed.
3. Any word or light that you may have been given needs to be confirmed through external circumstances, events or people—believers or unbelievers. God can speak to us again through anyone or anything as He chooses.
4. To seek godly counsel and witness in the spirit from mature God-fearing fellow Christians, especially those elderly saints who know the Lord and have walked in the Spirit.

Guided by these four principles, any decision you make in your life should be in line with the perfect and acceptable will of God. Remember, what is really important is not whether you make the right decision, it is that you deliberately choose God's will over your own will, you want Jesus to be the Lord of all over your life, family and business/career or ministry, and you want to do God's will in the best way you know how.

Jesus has promised, "Whoever has my commands and obeys them, he is the one who loves me. He who loves me will be loved by my Father, and I too will love him and show [or reveal] myself to him." (John

14:21) The beneficial result of knowing and doing the Lord's will is that Christ will reveal Himself to you—and to all those who truly love and obey Him. This is the highest reward that comes along with many other benefits from the practice of waiting on God. Remember that the Spirit says, "Without faith it is impossible to please God, because anyone who comes to Him must believe that He exists and that He rewards those who earnestly seek Him."

Chapter Six

WAITING ON GOD: THE ROLE OF THE HOLY SPIRIT

✠ ✠ ✠

THE PRACTICE OF WAITING ON GOD CANNOT be successful without some understanding of the role of the Holy Spirit. In order for this exercise to yield the desired results, we need to know the crucial role the Holy Spirit plays in the life of Christians both as individuals and as the body of Christ. We need to know who is the Holy Spirit and why He has been given to us so that we may without fail reap the promised fruit from this blessed practice.

Who Is the Holy Spirit?

The Greek word for the Holy Spirit is "parakletos" or the variation of "paraclete," which has been variously translated into English as the Comforter, Counselor, Helper, Advocate, Intercessor, Encourager, Strengthener and Standby. The Chinese rendition of "*Bao Hui Shi*" or "*Xun Wei Shi*" has these additional connotations: the Keeper, Protector, Grace-giver and Teacher/Instructor.

The Holy Spirit indeed is the soul and life of the church, which is the body of Christ, "the fullness of Him who fills all in all." (Ephesians 1:23NKJV) The Church of Christ, comprising all born-again Christians, should be so filled with the Holy Spirit that she may truly reflect "the fullness of Him who fills all in all." Christ—the Anointed One—is indeed our "all in all!" The Holy Spirit has been sent primarily to guide us into this profound truth: "*Christ is all in all.*"

The Holy Spirit is often referred to as the third Person in the Godhead—God the Father, God the Son, and God the Spirit—the Holy Trinity. Yet, of the three Persons in the Godhead, God the Spirit is probably the least known and recognized. So when we talk about the Holy Spirit, we are *not* talking about "someone" or "something" that is apart or separate from God; we *are* talking about God the Spirit—God Himself.

Likewise, when we talk about knowing God, we are talking about knowing God not just as God the Father and God the Son Jesus Christ, but also as God the Holy Spirit or else our knowledge of God is only two-thirds and, therefore, incomplete. We should seek to know God in *all* His fullness and completeness.

The Lord Jesus tells us in plain English: "God is Spirit, and His worshipers [i.e. those related to God] must worship in spirit and in truth." The Apostle Paul also emphatically states, "Now the Lord is the Spirit." (John 4:24; 2 Corinthians 3:17a)

As God's children, we are privileged to have been given the Holy Spirit who in His multiple role always works on our behalf, in our interest and for our benefit. "For I know the plans I have for you," declares the Lord, "plans to prosper you and not to harm you, plans to give you hope and a future." (Jeremiah 29:11) The blessed Holy Spirit has come to *bless* us and, more significantly, to *dwell* within us so that He may help us in every area of our lives, particularly in our personal relationship with God.

God Does Everything By His Spirit

We all recognize that God the Father and God the Son are both in heaven, Jesus being exalted at the right hand of the Father. In the physical realm, there is no way we on earth can reach out and touch God the Father and God the Son in heaven; the only way we can relate to God is through the Holy Spirit who, being the third Person in the Godhead, *is* God Himself. So God the Holy Spirit is the One with whom we can communicate, interact and feel close to in a personal and experiential way.

Another important point to bear in mind is this: Everything God does in and through us is done by His Holy Spirit—and through His Holy Word. The Spirit of God and the Word of God are inseparable; they always go hand in hand.

In the beginning, God created the universe by His Word and His Spirit. Today God converts and saves sinners by His Spirit through the Word—the Gospel. God dwells in us by His Spirit. God speaks to us by His Spirit through His inspired Word. God comforts, encourages, and strengthens us by His Word and the Holy Spirit.

The Spirit of God quickens the Word of God and causes it to be alive and makes it meaningful in our personal lives. God teaches and enlightens us by His Spirit through His Word. God energizes and empowers us by His Spirit. God heals us by the power of His Spirit and His Word. Above all, God changes us by His Spirit and the Word. Whatever God does, He does it by His Holy Spirit in conjunction with His Holy Word.

Therefore, in any fruitful practice of waiting on God, it is important to understand that we do not rely on our own efforts but wholly on the wonder-working power and the inner workings of the Holy Spirit—and through the Word of God.

To lead and guide us into all the Biblical truths—and into a deeper and fuller knowledge of the Holy Trinity—is largely the work of the Holy Spirit. Our job is simply to trust and obey God the Holy Spirit as we wait upon the Lord. We may not fully understand how the Holy Spirit works within us, but we can trust Him wholeheartedly for He always has our best interest at heart.

THE CENTRAL ROLE OF THE HOLY SPIRIT

The central role of the Holy Spirit, apart from revealing and glorifying the Lord Jesus, is to usher us into the conscious presence of God in order to establish a personal relationship—and bring about a spiritual union—with God so that we may know Him in all His fullness in a personal intimate way. Our God the Father, being a living and personal God, desires that we as His children have a close personal relationship with Him and that we are led consistently by His Spirit and guided unerringly by His Word.

The Bible clearly teaches that the Holy Spirit has been given to us so that we may have a personal relationship with God, a relationship so wonderful that it becomes a virtual union with Him. The Apostle John says, "No one has ever seen God….[But] we know that we live in Him and He in us, because He has given us of His Spirit." (1 John 4:12-13)

"We live in Him and He in us"—truly a mysterious union between God and human beings that has now been made possible because of the Holy Spirit given to us freely by God. What a wonderful relationship we can have with God through the Holy Spirit, though it seems incomprehensible from the human standpoint! How grateful we should be for the precious gift of the Holy Spirit!

Prior to His ascension, Jesus said of the Holy Spirit: "I will ask the Father, and He will give you another Counselor to be with you forever—the Spirit of truth. The world cannot accept Him, because it neither sees Him nor knows Him. But you know Him, for He lives with you and will be [or is] in you. I will not leave you as orphans; I will come to you. Before long, the world will not see me anymore, but you will see me [i.e. in the Person of the Holy Spirit]. Because I live [in you by the Spirit], you also will live." (John 14:16-19) Today we have this Jesus—the all-powerful and ever-present Helper in the Person of the Holy Spirit—living in us! He is indeed our "*all in all*"!

The Holy Spirit Unites Us To The Trinity

The Holy Spirit has been given to us for the primary purpose of bringing us into that wonderful union with the Holy Trinity—God the Father, God the Son and God the Holy Spirit. This is specifically taught by our Lord Jesus in Chapters 14 and 15 of the Gospel according to John. "At that day [meaning the day of Pentecost]," Jesus says, "you will know that I am *in* my Father, and you *in* Me, and I *in* you…Abide *in* Me, and I *in* you. He who abides *in* Me, and I *in* him, bears much fruit." (John 14:20, 15:4-5NKJV)

Seven times the word "in" is used in these few verses, signifying a true and complete union with the Holy Trinity! What a wonderful union between God and His people! It is through this mysterious union with God that we are miraculously transformed into the likeness of His Son Jesus Christ. And waiting on God is an essential part of the process whereby the Holy Spirit brings about this marvelous transformation and union with God in a way beyond human comprehension.

In order for the practice of waiting on God to be successful, we must do two things: 1. Read and meditate on the Word of God so as to allow God to speak to our hearts, 2. Trust in the wonder-working and life-changing power of the Holy Spirit as we allow Him to work freely within us.

Remember, God does everything by His Holy Spirit and through His Word. Whenever and wherever God does something, the Word of God and the Spirit of God are always at work hand in hand. The Apostle John tells us that there are three that testify: "The Father, the Word [that once became flesh] and the Holy Spirit, and these three are one." (John 5:7,8)

The Spirit of Wisdom and Revelation

The Holy Spirit is, of course, the Spirit of wisdom and revelation for which Paul prayed ceaselessly for the Christians at Ephesus "so that you may know Him better" and that "the eyes of your heart may be enlightened." (Ephesians 1:17-18) So the Holy Spirit brings revelation, enlightenment and understanding of Christ who is the mystery of God and of the things that God has prepared for those who love Him.

Concerning the revelatory role of the Holy Spirit, Paul writes, "No eye has seen, no ear has heard, no mind has conceived what God has prepared for those who love Him"—but God has *revealed* it to us by His Spirit. The Spirit searches all things, even the deep things of God…No one knows the thoughts of God except the Spirit of God." (1 Corinthians 2:9-10, 11b)

Jesus also says, "No one knows the Son except the Father, and no one knows the Father except the Son and those to whom the Son chooses to reveal Him." (Matthew 11:27b) In other words, no one can know God or Jesus Christ whom God has sent except through the revelation of the Holy Spirit. We may know a lot about the Bible and may have read all the books about knowing God, but unless we have "the Spirit of wisdom and revelation," we cannot truly know God.

No one can understand the things of God except by the revelation of the Holy Spirit. The mysteries of God are unveiled and made known to spiritual men and women only by the Spirit of God. As Paul explains, "The man [and woman] without the Spirit does not accept [or understand] the things that come from the Spirit of God, for they are foolishness to him [or her], and he [or she] cannot understand them because they are spiritually discerned [or revealed]."

But spiritual men and women who have and depend on the Holy Spirit can understand the mysteries of God only insofar as they are revealed by the Spirit. These are the people who, as Paul put it, "have not received the spirit of the world but the Spirit who is from God, that we may understand what God has freely given us."

Touching on the instructive and articulative role of the Holy Spirit, Paul states briefly, "This is what we speak, not in words taught us by human wisdom but in words taught by the Spirit, interpreting spiritual truths to spiritual men [and women]." (1 Corinthians 2:9-14)

Many Christians who love and serve the Lord with zeal and vigor seem to overlook one thing—probably the most important thing in a Christian's life—it is this: God delights to reveal His Son Jesus Christ in us, and the main reason that God has given us His Holy Spirit is to teach us everything we need to know about Jesus Christ. This He does for us by His Holy Spirit and through His Word especially when we take time to wait upon the Lord.

The Holy Spirit has come not only to give us power for service and ministry, but also, more importantly, to reveal Jesus Christ in all His fullness. "O that I may know Christ and the power of His resurrection" is the heart cry of many spiritual men and women! Therefore, we need to keep praying, as Paul did for the Ephesians, that God would grant us the Spirit of wisdom and revelation so that we may truly know Him and know Him better as time passes.

Holy Spirit: The Empowering Presence of God

The Holy Spirit is also the empowering presence of God in our lives; He is the One who strengthens us where we are weak and lifts us up when we are down, causing the power of God to be made perfect in our weaknesses. We know that during the Apostle Paul's prolonged trial, God said to him: "My grace is sufficient for you, for my power is made perfect in weakness." (2 Corinthians 12:9a)

As we learn to trust in the Holy Spirit and depend upon Him in every area of our lives, He will cause us to be united with the Almighty

God and eventually bring us to a place where we may be able to say with the apostle: "I can do everything through Him who gives me strength."(Philippians 4:13)

Holy Spirit: Our Greatest Teacher

The Holy Spirit is given to us also as our Teacher/Instructor. He is indeed the greatest Teacher of all times! Of the Holy Spirit being the Teacher, Jesus said, "The Counselor, the Holy Spirit, will teach you all things and will remind you of everything I have said to you." (John 14:26)

The Apostle John used the term "anointing" to describe the role of the Holy Spirit as the divine Teacher in a Christian's life. He writes, "As for you, the anointing [i.e. the indwelling Spirit] you received from Him remains in you, and you do not need anyone to teach you. But as the anointing *teaches you about all things…"* (1 John 2:27)

It is such a great privilege to be taught by the Holy Spirit who is God Himself. Let us believe that the Holy Spirit will fulfill His role as our Teacher/Instructor when we come to wait on the Lord.

Paul also speaks of the difference between being "taught by human wisdom" [or human intellect] and being "taught by the Spirit" [or divine wisdom]. There is, of course, also a distinction between being taught by the Spirit and being instructed only by the Scripture. We do well to take note of both of these differences.

We should labor to become men and women not only of the Word but of the Spirit as well. Waiting on the Lord, led by the Holy Spirit and instructed by the Holy Bible, is one effectual way of being taught by both the Word and the Spirit of God. The Holy Spirit has much yet to reveal to us from the Word of God as He teaches us about the things of God.

Jesus said to His disciple, "I have much more to say to you, more than you can now bear [or understand]. But when the Spirit of truth comes, He will guide you into all truth." (John 16:14, 13a) There is much yet to be learned about what God has in store for those who love Him. May the Lord help all of us to be good students in the School of the Holy Spirit.

As we take time to wait upon the Lord in silence, and read, meditate and pray over the Word of God, the Holy Spirit will certainly make

Jesus Christ more real and precious to our hearts and souls, and He will teach us the things that we need to know according to our respective spiritual capacities. The Holy Spirit is such a wonderful Teacher!

Knowing how much we can take, the Holy Spirit knows how to reach us on our own level, teaching us only the things we need to know at any given time. But we can count on the Holy Spirit to take us to a higher level of spiritual understanding as we keep up the practice of waiting on God.

The Anointing of the Holy Spirit

Much has been said about the anointing of the Holy Spirit. The anointing is being sought by many a Christian. According to the Apostle John, those of us who have received the Holy Spirit from God already have the anointing in us, and that anointing not only remains in us but also teaches us in all spiritual matters.

But what is the anointing of the Holy Spirit? How do we recognize it?

The anointing of the Holy Spirit, in short, is the impact or substantive manifestation of the presence of God the Spirit. It is, in effect, a divine Presence, often accompanied by the working of a supernatural power. It often comes with a soothing and healing effect, sometimes with a sense of sweetness and deliciousness. It is the intangible operation or activity of the Spirit of God in and through a Spirit-filled believer or minister. It is a holy and precious gift of God.

The anointing of the Holy Spirit carries with it not only the healing power of God but also the soul-saving and life-changing power of the Almighty. It is the uplifting and liberating power of the Spirit of God that can set people free from the shackles of sin or, for that matter, from any bondage, as the Scripture says, "The yoke shall be destroyed because of the anointing." (Isaiah 10:27dKJV)

The anointing of the Holy Spirit can be felt, and when you do feel it, you know that it is God the Spirit touching you and blessing you. Usually it is because of your obedience or faith that pleases God.

The anointing of the Holy Spirit also represents a seal—a stamp of approval—favor, good pleasure and certification of God. For instance, Jesus said of Himself, "On Him God the Father has placed His seal of approval" (John 6:27c), meaning that Jesus is the One favored, chosen, sent, empowered and certified by God the Father. As Peter declared, "Salvation is found in no one else, for there is no other name [than that of Jesus] under heaven given to men by which we must be saved." (Acts 4: 12)

The anointing of the Holy Spirit is extremely precious and desirable; it signifies God Himself being with you in your life and ministry or business. You can feel the anointing as it comes upon you and enables you to do things that you cannot do in your own strength, because it is the palpable and empowering presence of God.

Meanwhile, the measure of anointing will increase as you become more subject to the control of the Holy Spirit. Therefore, it is important that you learn to be led by the Holy Spirit as you wait on the Lord.

Where do we obtain the impartation of the anointing?

Well, if you have received the Holy Spirit—or the baptism of the Holy Spirit—the anointing is already in you. For the anointing to increase, however, you may have to go through some fiery trials as allowed or appointed by God. John the Baptist tells us that Jesus Christ is the One who "baptizes with the Holy Spirit and *fire*!"

Make no mistake about it. Christ—the Anointed One—is the Source of anointing. It is Christ who gives the Spirit and imparts the anointing, even though He may at times choose to do so through the laying on of hands. Moreover, "God gives the Spirit [or the anointing] without limit." (John 3:34b)

It is vitally important that we learn to live a life of abiding in the Lord—to remain attached to the One who is the Source of anointing and all other blessings. The practice of waiting on God, if carried on regularly and faithfully, will help us achieve this noble goal—constantly abiding in Christ.

THE ANOINTING FOR PUBLIC MINISTRY

The anointing of the Holy Spirit is given to the church and certain chosen ministers of God for the purpose of public ministry—preaching, teaching, prophesying, healing, and evangelizing. For this reason, every ministry and service of the church should and must bear the anointing of the Holy Spirit, just as everything used in the Tabernacle had to be sanctified with holy oil, a symbol of the Holy Spirit. By the same token, every anointed ministry and anointed servant of God is to be honored and accepted.

However, the measure of anointing given to each minister varies according to his/her calling. The greater the ministry, the greater is the anointing. God who calls also anoints—He knows what He is doing. For those of us who are called into the ministry—whatever our calling or the size of our ministry—we must have the anointing of the Holy Spirit. For it signifies God's commission, approval, and authorization, without which there is no true ministry to speak of. Equally indispensable is a thorough knowledge of the Word of God.

How can we minister without the knowledge of the Word of God and the anointing of the Holy Spirit? We do not minister in our own strength and with our own natural resources. Paul says, "Not that we are competent in ourselves to claim anything for ourselves, but our competence comes from God. He has made us competent as ministers of a new covenant—not of the letter but of the Spirit." (2 Corinthians 3:5-6)

We do well to remember what the Lord Himself said, "Apart from me, you can do nothing." Remember also what God said to Zerubbabel, "Not by might nor by power, but by my Spirit." (Zechariah 4:6)

One of the great benefits of waiting on God is the ever-increasing measure of the anointing of the Holy Spirit—for both our private life and public ministry—if we would deliberately allow the Holy Spirit to lead and teach us as we wait upon the Lord. If you do so, consequently, you will find yourself walking in the Spirit or living in the presence of God. In the meantime, the measure of anointing *in* and *upon* you will increase even without your knowing it.

Chapter Seven

THE POWER OF WAITING ON GOD: A PERSONAL TESTIMONY

✠ ✠ ✠

THE PRACTICE OF WAITING ON GOD HAS been a life-changing experience for me. When I first started this spiritual exercise some 40 years ago, I did not have any inkling as to its potential value and promised return in the long run. However, as a result of my waiting upon the Lord consistently over these many years, I can honestly say that I have become a better Christian man—a better husband, a better father and a better minister of the Gospel—amazingly with hardly any effort on my part. Waiting on God has also given me new insights and increasing power for Christian living and ministry! For these and many other intangible gains, I give God the glory for He has done it all!

Spiritual Crisis Paid Off

I was thrust into the practice of waiting on God by a major spiritual crisis in my earlier Christian life. There was a split in our church, and it was absolutely devastating! The split was caused by differences over leadership succession. It also led to the break-up of many affiliated churches. I thought that our family had joined the "best church" in the world; but because of what happened, I became utterly disappointed with the church and its people! For reasons unknown to us, the people who used to love us dearly suddenly turned against us. My wife and I were left confused, heartbroken, and dumbfounded. We did not know what to make of it. I was in total despair! Needless to say, the schism brought disgrace to the name of the Lord.

This was actually my second such experience since I became a Christian. But this one was much more devastating, leaving all our hopes and dreams in shambles! I had quit my well-paid secular job in response to a call into the ministry. We had literally "sold" all our possessions in order to serve the Lord full time in that missionary church, and we were gladly living by faith. I was on fire for God, ready to "go into all the world and preach the good news to all creation!" (Mark 16:15) Even our oldest eleven-year-old son once said, "When I grow up, I want to be a preacher!"

Following this painful experience, I had so many questions on my mind that I did not know where to go to find the answers. I was so discouraged that I did not want to go to any church any more or, for that matter, talk to anybody about the church. My faith was badly shaken, if not lost altogether. I kept asking the Lord: "Why, Lord, do you allow such things to happen in your church?"

I had to return to my journalistic profession to provide for my then family of six. Since there was no one who could help us out, I chose to stay home and pray after work and on weekends. We had actually quit going to church altogether. This was the backdrop against which I began the practice of waiting on God, although I did not have any teaching along this line. I walked into this unknown territory completely "cold," so to speak. The idea of waiting on the Lord was totally foreign to me. I was driven to my knees by the crisis, hoping to find help in time of need.

Initial Practice of Waiting on God

My initial approach to waiting on God was very simple. When I came home from work, oftentimes tired or nearly exhausted, I would go to our bedroom and shut the door behind me; I just wanted to be quiet and alone by myself. My loving and understanding wife, Nancy, would take our four children out for a walk or to play in a nearby park so I could have some peace and rest. I would sit still in a comfortable chair or get down on my knees, with my eyes closed, my head resting on my arms, always with an open Bible placed in front of me.

I was there only because I wanted to have some peace and rest after a long day's work. I did not know what it meant to wait on God or to be in the presence of God, nor did I know what to pray over the post-split situation, because I was so confused and frustrated, but I would read the Bible leisurely and sometimes haphazardly, hoping to find some answers to my questions. When I was too tired to read or pray, I just dozed off. But as soon as I woke up, I would resume reading or praying in silence. If I was waiting on the Lord or being in the presence of God, I was completely unaware of it. But I thoroughly enjoyed the quiet and peaceful atmosphere in the room. This, I did everyday for nearly two years, each time lasting for an hour or two.

Wonderful Things Happened

Lo and behold! Wonderful things happened! I began to discover changes inside of me. I cannot tell you exactly what transpired during these quiet times, but I realized that my worldview, value system, and attitude underwent a subtle change! For one thing, all my doubts and questions went away! My hidden anger and bitterness were gone! My emotional hurt and wounds were healed. No more pain! No more unforgiving! No more struggling! My heart was revived. My spirit was renewed. I was able to forgive and forget, almost as if nothing had happened! My love for Jesus was rekindled! My desire to follow and serve the Lord was restored.

Wow! God did so much for me, I marveled. Jesus is so wonderful! I never expected that investing one hour or more daily in the practice of waiting on God over just short of a two-year period could have produced so much "windfall" profit! Yet, this was only the beginning of what might be called a "new world" experience!

After a long absence from church, we started meeting with a small group of new Christian friends at a private home. Our necessary fellowship with other believers was thus resumed.

All Things Work Together for Our Good

Talk about the word of God being powerful. The one single Scripture verse that seemed to answer all my questions, once and for all, is this: "And we know that all things work together for good to those who love

God, to those who are the called according to His purpose." (Romans 8:28NKJV) Yes, "all things"—good or bad from our human point of view—are meant to work for our benefit as long as we love the Lord.

As I began to see the truthfulness of this familiar verse, I stopped complaining! Instead, I started thanking and praising God for everything that God had allowed to happen in my life, even for the unpleasant things, because He made me to know that "all things work together for good to those who love God."

These were some of the initial results of my waiting on God in the first two years. Looking back, I must say that it was God who in His great mercy brought me into "the secret place of the Most High" in time to meet my critical need as well as to teach me something about the power of waiting on God. As the psalmist writes profoundly, "He who dwells in the secret place of the Most High shall abide under the shadow of the Almighty." (Psalm 91:1NKJV)

Nevertheless, by this time, I still did not quite understand what waiting on the Lord was all about, nor did I really appreciate the vital importance of being in the presence of God. But I began to study the Scriptures in order to gain some understanding of this precious truth while I carried on my daily practice of waiting on God. (See Chapter One: "What the Bible Says About Waiting On God.")

First Missionary Trip Overseas

Shortly after I experienced these changes in my Christian life, I was led to go to Singapore on my first missionary trip. I knew some Christian brothers there, but none of them had invited me. The Lord just laid it on my heart to go forth in faith. After I paid for my airfare, I had very little money left in my pocket. I did not know where I was going to stay in Singapore. But I told the Lord that I was prepared to sleep on the street, if necessary, since Singapore is a tropical city-state.

Upon my arrival in Singapore, I made contact with a brother who introduced me to a well-to-do Chinese family where I was warmly received as a guest and stayed for one month! During this period, God surprised me by opening doors for me to minister in a number of Chinese churches in Singapore, including the one that sprang from Watchman Nee's "little flock" movement in China during the first part of the last century.

REVIVAL IN SINGAPORE

To my great surprise and astonishment, a revival broke out unexpectedly in this last church where I ministered nightly for about one week. At the end of the last service, as I recall, dozens of people rushed to the front in response to an altar call, weeping and repenting of their lukewarmness and other sins. An elderly Chinese woman, who had been with that church since its beginning, said to me afterward: "I have never seen anything like it!"

I marveled at all that God had done on this trip! I was particularly amazed that God allowed me to experience the anointing and the power of the Holy Spirit on my very first missionary trip in a way I had never known before! I wondered if this was one of the results of my waiting upon the Lord. Little did I know that the trip to Singapore was only the beginning of many overseas missionary journeys that were to take place in subsequent years!

During the following year, I traveled to Taiwan where I met providentially a man who was living in the presence of God all the time! His name was Hans H. Waldvogel, a Swiss-born German-speaking American pastor from Brooklyn, New York. For many years he had been teaching his people to wait on the Lord, to be men and women of prayer, and to walk circumspectly in the presence of God. He was in Taiwan holding a crusade, and I was his Chinese interpreter.

In the church that Pastor Waldvogel founded in New York, an unusual sign hanging at the head of the stairway to the lower auditorium says, "Please, before speaking to anyone, talk to God upon your knees." This is characteristic of his teachings on the inner life.

I noticed that this American pastor was practicing what he was preaching. He lost no time in waiting on the Lord. During the two weeks I spent with him, I saw in this man an exemplary minister who was living in the presence of God day and night; he was in constant unbroken fellowship with Jesus. I said to myself, "He's like Brother Lawrence," known for his book, *"The Practice of the Presence of God."* If there was a man in America today who lived in God twenty-four hours a day seven days a week, I thought, it was Pastor Waldvogel. His one message was: "Nothing is important but abiding in Jesus."

Pastor Waldvogel's teachings along these lines and the conversations I had with him during those days confirmed my findings that waiting on the Lord and constantly abiding in Christ is the right way to go! The way this man walked with God and how he moved and ministered in the power of the Holy Ghost deeply impressed me, and it has had a lasting impact on my own spiritual life and ministry!

Hans Waldvogel went to be with the Lord in 1969 shortly before my family and I moved to Washington, D. C. because of my job assignment. Later, I visited his church in New York and met his nephew, the Reverend Edwin H. Waldvogel who is the current senior pastor, and ministers from the other churches of the Ridgewood Fellowship. Our association with the Fellowship has greatly benefited our spiritual lives as well as those of the Chinese church that later came into being in Maryland.

More Intensive Waiting On God

In January 1985, I resigned from my secular position and returned to full-time ministry, living by faith again. This was five years after we started the Chinese Christian Church of Maryland and the Southwest Federal Prayer Fellowship in Washington, D. C., the latter being an all-American group comprising federal government employees.

Freed from secular occupation, and with a growing desire to know Christ better, I decided to devote additional time to the practice of waiting on God. For the ensuing five years, I managed to spend four hours each morning five days a week waiting on the Lord. I did this, for the most part, in silence and stillness. I felt I was being brought to a new dimension of waiting upon the Lord. I began to make new discoveries about the secret of being quiet and silent before the Lord. "Those who wait on the Lord shall renew their strength"—this particular Bible verse began to take on new meaning in my life.

I began to enjoy more greatly the wonderful presence of God. I never thought for one moment that spending four hours alone with God every morning was just too much or sheer boredom. As I waited on the Lord day after day and week after week, I became increasingly aware of God's presence in my life, of His great love for me, and of His peace and joy in my heart. I began to understand what David wrote, "In Your presence is fullness of joy; at Your right hand are pleasures forevermore." (Psalm 16:11b) I found that there is nothing more satisfying and rewarding than being in the presence of the Lord.

Oftentimes the room where I usually sat still and quiet before the Lord was filled with such peace and tranquility as if it were a holy place. This was indeed a "sacred" silence—the intangible evidence of the presence of God. There were times when I was so filled with the joy of the Lord that I had to get up and pace up and down, worshiping and praising God!

Sometimes I found myself joyfully "dancing" in the Spirit, thanking God for His great love, mercy, and wonderful presence in my heart and life! God the Holy Spirit made Himself so real to me! God the Son Jesus Christ became increasingly precious and sweet to my soul! Phrases like "He is the lily of the valley," "He is the bright and morning star" and "He is the fairest of ten thousand in my soul" began to take on new meaning in my personal relationship with Christ.

Deeper Into the Word of God

There were other times when I was studying the Scriptures, I was consciously led by the Holy Spirit back and forth between the New and Old Testaments, deep into the Word of God. It seemed as though the Bible became a new and living book to me! My love and hunger for the Word of God was intensified as my understanding was being enlightened. The more I studied the Bible, the more I wanted to dig into it! It was like a newly-found "gold mine!" There were times I felt like "feasting" on the Word of God—the manna from heaven!

There were also times when I was literally "soaked" in the presence of God; I was so absorbed in the Word of God that I was completely ignorant of what was going on outside of my prayer room. Four hours of waiting upon the Lord went by so quickly!

As a result of my waiting upon the Lord, I became increasingly appreciative of the completeness of the Bible as a whole and of the soundness of the Christian doctrine. I was reminded time and again that I must not take the Scripture out of context, that I must study and teach the Bible in its entirety, and that I must not deviate from its Center—Jesus Christ who is the Savior of the world!

Understanding and Interpreting the Word of God

During my quiet times alone with God, I learned that the Holy Spirit is the original Author of the Scriptures, although the sixty-sixty books and epistles—thirty-nine in the Old Testament and twenty-seven in the New Testament—were written at different times in history by "holy men of God as they were moved [or inspired] by the Holy Spirit."

There are always some Scripture passages or verses that are difficult to understand, but if we try to interpret them according to our own will and understanding, thereby distorting or twisting the Word of God, it will only result in our "own destruction" as the Apostle Peter has warned. (2 Peter 1:21, 3:16NKJV)

Only the Holy Spirit—the original Author of the Scriptures—is the illuminator and the most authoritative interpreter of the Bible. In other words, in trying to understand the Word of God correctly, we do not lean on our own understanding, we must rely on the Holy Spirit for enlightenment as well as for proper interpretation and application of the Scriptures. This is one of the purposes of the practice of waiting on God—so that God may teach us directly from His Word. Jesus has told us that the Holy Spirit has come to "guide you into all truth!"

As I kept up the practice of waiting on God, the Scripture passages or verses that did not make sense to me before, suddenly or gradually became meaningful and helpful not only to me personally but also to the people to whom I was called to minister and teach! Yes, the Holy Spirit has come to be our Helper not only in the understanding and application of the Scriptures but also in all other areas of our lives!

Not only was my understanding of the Scriptures enlightened during the years of waiting upon the Lord, but I also found—to my great delight and surprise—that some of the passages or verses that I read and meditated upon had been firmly planted or "written" in my heart—apparently by the indwelling Holy Spirit! I did not realize it until God opened new doors for my ministry at home and abroad.

For instance, as I was speaking in the first of many conferences in Taiwan in the 1990s, the anointing of the Holy Spirit came upon me in a surprisingly new way, and the word of the Lord came literally gushing forth from my mouth even without my thinking about them! Some of the Bible verses I read before just flowed out so swiftly that I could hardly contain them! Amazed, I asked myself, "Where did these words come from?" Then I realized that they had been "written" on my heart by the Spirit of the Lord!

Speaking of His people in New Testament times, the Lord said, "I will put my laws in their minds and write them on their hearts." (Hebrews 8:10b) Jesus, foretelling His disciples about the ministry of the Holy Spirit in the New Testament era, said, "The Counselor, the Holy Spirit, whom the Father will send in my name, will teach you all things and will *remind* you of everything I have said to you." (John 14:26)

Greater Anointing of the Holy Spirit

Speaking of the greater anointing that had come upon me, I believe the additional impartation had taken place during the preceding years of my waiting upon the Lord even without my knowing it. This was apparently part of God's preparation for my traveling ministry that was to take place later on.

I found out by experience that prolonged waiting on God will also bring increasing anointing of the Holy Spirit because when you are waiting on God, you are actually connected to Christ—the Anointed One—who dispenses and baptizes with the Holy Spirit and fire! Your anointing will increase automatically as long as you are connected to the Anointed One. This requires the incessant practice of waiting on God.

Jesus says, "If a man remains in me and I in him, he will bear much fruit," part of that fruit is the anointing of His Holy Spirit. The Bible also tells us, "God gives the Spirit [or the holy anointing] without limit." (John 15:5b; 3:34b) In other words, God will give you as much of the Spirit—or the anointing of the Holy Spirit—as you desire and as your capacity allows. As you keep up the practice of waiting on God, He will enlarge your capacity so that you can be filled with more of His Spirit; the more you wait on the Lord, the greater will be your anointing!

Not only has God enlarged my spiritual capacity during the years of my waiting on the Lord, but He has also expanded the scope of my ministry with an added measure of the anointing. I have found this, to my grateful surprise, to be the case during my extensive travels here in the United States and overseas.

The Inner Life Strengthened

God's word says, "Those who wait on the Lord *shall* renew their strength." Waiting upon the Lord is God's way of strengthening our inner life, a mighty work done internally by the indwelling Holy Spirit. This is what the Apostle Paul prayed for the people of God: "That out of His glorious riches He may strengthen you with power through His Spirit in your inner being, so that Christ may dwell in your hearts through faith." (Ephesians 3:16,17a)

The reality of Christ dwelling in my heart through faith became increasingly true as I continued to learn from the Holy Spirit while waiting on the Lord. Today whenever I think of the resurrected Christ living in my heart, I cannot help but feel energized and uplifted!

I have found that Christ is not only my spiritual life but also the sustaining strength of my physical life. Since I started the practice of waiting on God forty years ago, the good Lord has not allowed me to suffer from any sickness or disease except for an occasional bout with flu or cold. I did have some minor problems in my body over the years, but they have been healed naturally in time. I have tried to eat right, exercise regularly, and sleep adequately. On the whole, I must say that God has blessed me with excellent health, for which I am always grateful.

While I have benefited physically from the rest I have had while waiting on God, I have been especially strengthened spiritually as well as emotionally. In other words, I have been made strong in my soul, spirit and body! I used to be a quick-tempered person and have had long struggles in this area; but since I started the practice of waiting on God, I have found myself increasingly slow to anger because of the growing inner strength that comes from waiting on the Lord! God has also delivered me from my other emotional weaknesses! I can say now that I have been empowered to handle my emotions and reactions!

During these years of waiting on the Lord, I have found God to be the sole Source of my strength—spiritual, emotional and physical strength. Moreover, I have found Him to be the Source of wisdom, love, peace, joy and rest. Since I started the practice of waiting on God, I have been blessed with increasing inner peace and inner rest, as the Bible describes it, "the peace of God which surpasses all understanding." (Philippians 4:7NKJV) With this divine peace and rest in my heart,

I am now free from fear, worry or anxiety, no matter what happens in my life!

When I found myself lacking in wisdom, love or patience, I would just come to God and wait upon Him, expecting Him to meet my needs without fail. Sometimes God seems to have delayed answering my prayers, but He has always met my needs in a timely fashion. God has never sent me away empty-handed!

The Empowering Presence of God

There were times when I sat still and silent in God's presence—being connected to the Source of power—for extended periods of time, I became very conscious of God's power being imparted to me by the Holy Spirit within, and I just took it in by faith. I felt myself like a weak battery being plugged into a powerful charger; I was being charged up! I believed with all my heart that I was being renewed and strengthened in my inner being because I came away feeling refreshed and uplifted!

There were other times when I clearly sensed the presence of God permeating the entire room where I was sitting alone. There was absolute silence—a holy silence; I sat there motionless, with my eyes closed, but I knew in my heart that it was the powerful presence of the Lord! Amazingly, it was in the presence of God that I was changed! There is something wonderful about the presence of God, especially about silence before God, that I cannot explain, but it has done wonders for me!

There were also times, however, when I felt or sensed nothing at all during my waiting on the Lord, but I still believed in my heart that I was in the presence of God. Although I did not do anything on my own, I discovered afterward that God has indeed changed me, and He has strengthened me inwardly with the power of His Holy Spirit! In this particular way, God has taught me and enabled me to live a victorious Christian life through the power of the indwelling Holy Spirit! I am often reminded of what the Lord Jesus said, "Apart from me, you can do nothing."

I can go on and on testifying to the power of waiting on God! In summing up, I would like to leave you, my dear reader, with these closing thoughts:

>The greatest benefit I have received from years of waiting on the Lord is two-fold: An increasing knowledge of God and a deepening personal relationship with Him. I consider this to be the most important thing and the greatest gain in any Christian's life.

>There is nothing more restful, rewarding and satisfying than to be in the presence of the Almighty God. Remember this: "He who dwells in the secret place of the Most High shall abide under the shadow of the Almighty." The practice of waiting on God will help us to find out for ourselves what it means to be in the presence of God—"the secret place of the Most High."

>The most wonderful thing about the practice of waiting on God is that you do not have to do anything in your own strength; God will do everything for you in His own powerful way. All you need is a simple child-like faith as you come into the presence of God, and He will teach you everything you need to know about this life and the life to come.

>After I started the practice of waiting upon the Lord, I was never the same again. Frankly, I never thought that waiting on God the way the Bible teaches could change a person's life.

>The countless hours I have spent alone with God were the most rewarding and edifying times in my Christian life! The impact of these quiet times with God upon both my life and ministry has been greater than all the external church activities and conferences I have attended combined.

>What God has done for me and in me during these years of waiting on the Lord has been far beyond my expectation and comprehension. To this date I am still discovering the things that God has planted or "set" in my soul, the main thing being God's abiding presence! Oh, the power of waiting on God! Oh, the secret of being in His presence!

>If I have learned anything practical about self-denial or dying to the self, it was imparted to me by the Holy Spirit during my long hours of waiting on the Lord and meditating upon the Word of God.

>If I have gained any understanding of what it means to walk in the Spirit or live in the presence of God, it was granted to me during these many years of my waiting upon the Lord.

>If I have learned anything about living a life of abiding in Christ as every Christian should, the abiding grace was given to me, even

without my knowing it, while I waited on the Lord over a protracted period of time.

>For the first seventeen years of my Christian life, I knew little or nothing about the paramount importance of knowing and doing the will of God. Since I started the practice of waiting on God, however, I have been made to understand how important it is for God's people to know and live according to the will of God!

>Since I came to know the Holy Spirit as my personal Teacher/ Instructor, I stopped running around seeking merely human wisdom and counsel. I found this teaching of Apostle John to be so true: "As for you [meaning Spirit-indwelled, mature Christians], the anointing you received from Him remains in you, and you do not need anyone to teach you. But as His anointing teaches you about all things…remain [or abide] in Him." (1 John 2:27)

>The various things that the Holy Spirit has taught me during my quiet times have actually come from the Lord Jesus who said, "When the Spirit of truth comes, He will guide you into all truth. He will not speak on His own; He will speak only what He hears. He will bring glory to me by taking from what is mine and making it known to you." (John 16:13-14)

>The God who dwells in us by His Spirit also guides and teaches us by His Spirit. After nearly forty years of waiting upon the Lord, I am still learning from the Holy Spirit—whom I cherish as the greatest Teacher of all time—who has much yet to reveal to us.

>Once you have entered into "the secret place of the Most High" God who is already in you, and have "tasted and seen that the Lord is good," you will not exchange it for anything in this world. You *will* slowly but surely enter in—be ushered into the wonderful presence of God—and be changed into the likeness of Jesus Christ if you make waiting on the Lord a matter of life-long practice!

Appendix 1

WAITING ON GOD……

BY MARTHA W. ROBINSON

✣ ✣ ✣

SECOND CORINTHIANS 3:18 (REVISED VERSION) SAYS, "BUT we all with unveiled face, *reflecting* as in a mirror the *glory of the Lord,* are transformed into the same image from *glory* to *glory*."

If we looked at *Jesus more*, and ourselves, our friends, our trials, our failures, conditions of life, and the world, flesh and devil *less*, we would *reflect His* image more and more; the hardness, impurity, temper, and selfishness would fade away, and there would be tenderness, purity, gentleness, and love just taking their places—changing from glory to glory.

This is why He requires closet prayer. This is why we need to get still before Him and listen to His voice—get into His presence. If we *listened* to Him more, looked to Him in stillness more, and chattered less to Him, we would get the sense of His presence better.

Whenever you can, take a few minutes of just waiting on Jesus, not necessarily praying, but just waiting, looking into His face, desiring His presence. At first, you may not seem to receive much, but if you take every opportunity, presently your soul will hunger for Him, and the sweetness of Himself will come to you, and you will get [become] like lovers—[you will] rather slip away with Him just for a minute or two than to talk or read or rest or eat. When you are tired, or rushed, or nervous, a few minutes with Him in the stillness of His presence will rest you more than anything in the world.

"If any man [or woman] *thirst*, let him [or her] come to Me," Jesus said. You are thirsty for righteousness, for a work to be done in you, but you must have the righteousness of *Christ*. (See Philippians 3:9)

Don't bother your head as to the details of being so clothed upon. After a square look at yourself and a real consecration, you are a vessel in God's hands, and you can just enjoy Jesus. Take all the time you have, all the thought you have to spare, and follow on to *know* Jesus! He will supply *all* your need.

In your hurrying life, you can't split hairs. Let God have His way. Ask Him to make you hungry and thirsty for Jesus, and give Him the chance to answer by getting into His presence every opportunity you have, and *He* will give [you] the victory along every line.

I have learned in prayer to do less talking than I used to do. We rush into God's presence too boldly and irreverently. If, when we go to prayer, we would just take time in the beginning to get quiet in [the] soul, to be still before Him, then, when we do speak, first thank and praise Him; when we did offer our petitions, we would not so often have the feeling of their falling back on our heads unanswered, but we would pray "through."

Often, when I have a burden on me until it seems as if I can hardly stand it until I get before the Lord alone, and I expect to just lay my difficulties before Him in detail and with earnest supplication. When I follow this method of prayer, by the time I have felt His presence and felt His touch, and praised Him, I have just a sweet time of worship, and when I get up, I think, "Why, I never told the Lord about that at all"—and I just don't need to, the burden is gone, the problem solved, and I know He has undertaken for me.

Not that we never need to supplicate, because we do, but not so often as we sometimes think. But we need *far* more waiting on God than we have.

Appendix 2

INWARDNESS*......

BY MARTHA W. ROBINSON

✠ ✠ ✠

WHEN JESUS FIRST SETS VESSELS [OR SOULS] to love Him, He wants them to see Him all the time, every moment, and if they are very much in earnest, they live that way—moment by moment.

In the beginning of such experience, most of the time they pray, praise, wait on God, commune, and often, if at work, see Jesus in the soul.

If they grow in this experience and become vessels of God for His use, they begin to seek more for Him, and He comes more to them, for He does to all who seek Him from the heart.

Also, He begins to draw their thoughts all the time—every moment—to Himself, causing them to find Him within. This is the beginning of the inward or deeper life.

As soon as this change takes place, He then teaches, if He can make them to get it, either by teachers or by their light, how to "practice the presence of God"—that is, to keep the mind stayed on Jesus—each wandering thought, act, word or feeling being recalled (i.e., called back) by the will of the vessel in the love of God.

* This teaching was given with a solemn warning to those who were gifted and blessed and used of God, especially ministers, that they were not to become occupied with the blessings of God, particularly with the gifts and operations of the Holy Spirit, instead of with their Giver, and not to consider the manifest power of God more important than maintaining the presence of the Lord in one's life. For this contains the basic principles of a successful Christian life and ministry.

However, this takes care. Often the mind lingers over a subject not of God. Turn the mind back to God. Words come not appointed by Him. Check such words at once, as soon as remembered. Look within and tell Jesus He rules, you will act, think, and speak as He would, and He will look after you to help you to be like that.

Also, you need to watch and pray to be in God, wait in God, etc. To so live for a time makes the inward change to abide in anyone who will go down to thus live; but if you keep to this lowliness, rest, and faith to be all the time in God so, then the voluntary act of dwelling in God, seeing God, thinking of God, and keeping in is done altogether by the Holy Ghost, which is the true inwardness called for in every Christian.

ABOUT THE AUTHOR

✠ ✠ ✠

JACK K. CHOW, a journalist-turned pastor and author, has written five books on Christian spirituality, including "On Experiencing God," "The Christian Inward Life" and "What It Means To Be Filled with the Spirit"—all in his native Chinese. This is his first book in English in which he shares his insights and experience of walking with God. The author has traveled extensively in Southeast Asia, the United States, Canada and Europe as a conference speaker and seminar teacher. He and his wife Nancy, married for 53 years, have seven adult children and 15 grandchildren. They live in Dallas, Texas.